Timor-Leste Tour and Guide, East Timor

Tourism Information

Author
Peter Owen

SONITTEC PUBLISHING. All rights reserved. No part of this publication may be reproduced, distributed, or transmitted in any form or by any means, including photocopying, recording, or other electronic or mechanical methods, without the prior written permission of the publisher, except in the case of brief quotations embodied in critical reviews and certain other noncommercial uses permitted by copyright law. For permission requests, write to the publisher, addressed "Attention: Permissions Coordinator," at the address below.

Copyright © 2019 Sonittec Publishing
All Rights Reserved

First Printed: 2019.

Publisher:
SONITTEC LTD
College House, 2nd Floor
17 King Edwards Road,
Ruislip
London
HA4 7AE.

Table of Content

- Introduction 1
- **About Timor Leste** 4
  - *Geography & Climate* 4
  - *History* 6
  - *Economy* 8
  - *Nature & Wildlife* 11
  - *People & Culture* 14
    - Timor Leste Culture in more Detail 21
    - Perspectives 35
- **Travel and Tourism** 47
  - *Things to Do* 47
    - Arts & Crafts 49
    - Beaches 50
    - Birding 51
    - Diving 51
    - Coffee 53
    - Dolphins & Whales 54
    - Eating & Drinking 55
    - Fishing 56
    - Events & Festival 56
    - Heritage & Culture 57
    - Hiking & Walking 59
    - Local Markets 60
    - Mountain Biking 60
    - Surfing, Diving and Snorkeling 61
    - National Park 66
  - *Attractions* 67
    - Volunteering 69
  - *Destination* 70
    - Municipalities 70
      - Atauro (Dili) 71
      - Liquica 72
      - Covalima 73

    Ermera 73
    Baucau 75
    Bobonaro 76
    Dili 78
    Lautem 80
    Aileu 82
    Ainaro 83
    Manufahi 84
    Oecusse-Ambeno 86
    Manatuto 88
    Viqueque 89
Plan your Trip 91
    Arriving in Timor-Leste 91
    Getting Around 92
    Accommodation 97
    Safety & Health 107
    Visa & Immigration 109
Popular Locations 113
Food and Restaurants 119
Shopping and Leisure 122
Transportation 123
Travel Tips 125
Weather 127
Holidays and Festivals 128
Food of East Timor 130

Introduction

Timor Leste, Portuguese Timor, Timor Lorosa'e, East Timor the countless name changes say a lot about "Asia's newest country." Tucked in a little corner of Southeast Asia, northwest of Australia, East Timor is a secret paradise and an unsung tourist destination that is sure to grab any globetrotter's heart with its untouched mountains and beaches, plus its breathtaking biking and diving destinations. Despite being enslaved by colonization for years, the country is beginning to make a name for itself and is now frequented by visitors from neighboring Australia, the Lesser Sundra Islands and the Indonesian archipelago.

East Timor includes the eastern half of an island shared with Indonesia, the "Crocodile Island" of Timor and nearby Jaco, Atauro, and Oecusse. All 5,949 square miles (15,410 square-kilometers) have spectacular beaches, unrivaled dive sites, and untouched scenery, especially around Mount Ramelau, the best coasts. Admire shipwrecks while taking in the beautiful sunset backdrop over at Dili Harbor. East Timor has incredible potential for ecotourism, thanks to its natural beauty. Nino Konis National Park on the eastern outskirts of the country can easily pass as one of the world's richest tropical and coastal zones.

Since tourists are still few and far between, visitors to East Timor have the rare privilege of being the first to discover everything that the place has to offer: from its rich cultural heritage, stunning natural attractions, prehistoric archaeological sites, and even the remnants of its Indonesian and Portuguese colonial periods. Travelers are engulfed in the history as years of colonization and the struggle for independence are revealed.

If you are planning to visit, don't expect extravagant hotels and first class accommodation, but there are some good choices. Many of the hotels can be found in the capital town of Dili where the striking views and coastlines outweigh a lack of amenities. There are many creative options too, from camping to cheap guesthouses and even the option to stay in a convent, especially in the countryside. Seafood dishes are a definite favorite, especially in seaside towns. Nightlife is generally quiet, but there are inner-city restaurants, bars and nightclubs that stay open late.

Presidente Nicolau Lobato International Airport is the main international gateway to the country, located in Dili. Various carriers fly directly to the airport, mostly from Indonesia, Australia, and Singapore, from where connections to US can be made. Traveling by land from Indonesia is possible via the main land border at Mota'ain, some 70 miles (115 kms) from the capital. Cross-border buses will take you between East Timor and the town of Kupang in West Timor, but there are also non-direct buses that serve other cities.

Another great way to see the country is on one of the many cycling routes. There are scenic drives too, though some are arduous and tricky to navigate, but still car rental is an option. Taxis are easy to find around the capital and many destinations are hard to miss, like the country's highest peak, Mount Ramelau, Nino Konis National Park, and several dive sites, especially those around the Atauro and Jaco Islands.

Peter Owen

About Timor Leste
Geography & Climate

Location

Within South-East Asia, Timor-Leste (East Timor) lies 400km north of Australia, across the Timor Sea, and in the Lesser Sunda Islands at the eastern end of the Indonesian archipelago. It comprises the eastern half of Timor Island, the separate enclave of Oecusse, situated in West Timor and the small off-shore islands of Atauro and Jaco.

Land

Formed by continental uplift along a major fault line (and in the case of Atauro, submarine volcanic activity), Timor-Leste is extremely rugged with a mountainous backbone rising to over 2,000m. Even the highest peaks have marine fossils and the forested ranges are riddled with caves. Almost half of Timor-Leste's 15,000 sq/km land area has a slope of 40 degrees or more making it scenically beautiful but extremely difficult for road construction and cultivation. Steep terrain combined with inconsistent rainfall and stony, limestone soils are challenging for the farmers.

West of Baucau and around Lospalos and Maliana there are rolling highland plains important for agriculture. On the south side of Timor-Leste the coastal flats are 20-30km wide, while to the north they are much narrower with many stretches where the mountains fall directly into the sea. There are wild rocky headlands and long expanses of silky white sand beaches. Along both coasts views across the shimmering ocean are stunning. Timor-Leste's fringing reefs are extensive and rightly lauded.

Water

Most of Timor-Leste's large braided rivers completely disappear in the dry season, but after torrential rain can turn into raging torrents, sometimes flash flooding. Impressive waterfalls cascading down the mountain-sides can also be seen at this time.

Lake Ira Laloro is the only lake of any size. There are also smaller salt lakes and along the south coast marshes teeming with wildlife. Bubbling mud pools can be viewed in Oecusse and there are geothermal hot springs at Marobo, Waicana (near Venilale), Uato Carbau (near Viqueque) and on Atauro to name a few.

Climate

Timor-Leste has a hot tropical climate with a dry season, May-November, and a wet season, December-April. The temperature on the coast is usually between 25-35C and in the mountains at higher elevation it is much cooler sometimes wet and misty and at other times clear and invigorating.

There are many different micro-climates from dry barren hill sides to thickly forested peaks interspersed with cultivated areas. In general, as you drive south the countryside becomes much more lush and greener.

History
Ancient

Timor-Leste (East Timor) has a rich history and culture developed over centuries. Archeological evidence, including ancient rock art and stone carvings, indicate people have been living in Timor-Leste for over 4,000 years. The early Austronesian hunter-gather arrivals were later joined by Asian migrants who introduced agriculture. Over time, Timor-Leste became divided into a number of small kingdoms with skirmishes frequent between the differing tribal groupings.

Colonialism

From as early as the 13th century, there are records of visiting Javanese and Chinese traders drawn by sandalwood, honey and wax.

In the 15th century, both Dutch and Portuguese started arriving, eventually resulting in Timor-Leste becoming a Portuguese colony for over 400 years. While the Portuguese introduced coffee production, along with sugar cane and cotton, their rule was also a time of periodic bloody uprisings as they raised local taxes and used forced labour in construction plantations. Missionaries soon followed spreading the Catholic faith. As the colonists were mostly concerned with trading and for the best part concentrated their presence around the coast, the traditional lifestyle and animist beliefs of most Timorese remained relatively unchanged well into the 20th century.

WWII

The Japanese were the next invaders, occupying Timor-Leste during WWII, following the landing of Australian troops. 40-60,000 Timorese are estimated to have died as a result of horrific repression and associated starvation.

Indonesian Occupation

In 1975, after the Japanese defeat, withdrawal of the Portuguese and Timor–Leste's subsequent declaration of independence, Indonesia launched a full scale invasion. A 24 year period of 'pacification', costing the lives of more than 200,000 Timorese from violence and associated disease and famine followed. Spirited Timorese resistance and concerted efforts at the United Nations culminated in an independence referendum being held in 1999. Despite a bloody campaign of intimidation, an overwhelming 78.5% of Timorese bravely voted for independence.

In retaliation, the Indonesian army and backed militia rampaged through the country, torching Dili and other towns. Nationwide, it is estimated a further 1,000 2,000 civilians were massacred and around 70% of services, infrastructure and buildings were destroyed.

Independence

International peacekeepers eventually helped the Timorese restore peace and in 2002 the country regained its independence as the Democratic Republic of Timor-Leste, amidst huge celebrations. Since that time and with relative calm in recent years Timor-Leste's primary focus has been on national development.

Economy
Post-conflict

In 2002, Timor-Leste (East Timor) became an independent nation after more than four centuries of Portuguese colonial rule and two decades of Indonesian annexation. Since then the Government of Timor-Leste has been focused on retaining political unity and boosting economic growth. This is not an easy undertaking after the widespread violence, population displacement and property destruction the country experienced following the 1999 referendum. Most of its infrastructure was destroyed at that time including electrical, water and sewerage systems, roads, schools and medical facilities as well as public and private sector properties.

Despite the steady progress made to date, more than 40% of the population is estimated to still live below the poverty line and there is high unemployment.

Development

In addition to growth in Timor-Leste's public sector, an increasing number of small businesses, primarily in construction and in the wholesale and retail sale of goods, are being set up. Most of these private sector business enterprises are concentrated in Dili, which consequently has changed significantly since independence with ongoing construction of buildings and upgrading of infrastructure.

As in most capital cities, Dili offers a wide range of shopping, accommodation, restaurants and other services. In contrast, the towns and traditional villages in the surrounding districts have changed to a less noticeable extent, with the exception of road upgrading and electricity development. The people who live in rural areas continue to be primarily engaged in small scale fishing, forestry and farming.

Oil Sector

Currently Timor-Leste's economy is mostly dependent on the extraction of oil reserves from the Timor Sea which account for a massive 80% of GDP. These funds have enabled significant investment in core services and infrastructure, especially related to roads and electricity.

Other Sectors

Apart from the oil and gas revenue, coffee exports and net tourism receipts account for Timor-Leste's other main sources of foreign exchange. These, however, represent a small percentage of the country's import and service payments.

Together with several other sectors, the Government regards growth in tourism as critical to future economic development a goal to be achieved by taking advantage of the country's natural beauty, culture and heritage and by focusing on boutique, adventure and ecotourism experiences.

Improving production from agriculture and fishing is also seen as very important, especially from a food security perspective and as a way of reducing imports.

Nature & Wildlife

Vegetation

Timor-Leste (East Timor) still feels untamed with a wild natural beauty. In many places it seems untouched. Lying climatically in the dry tropics, vegetation varies widely from the damp lower lying southern plains, to the moist and much cooler mountain country and then to the dry north coast. As a result of the differing micro-climates the vegetation changes quickly as you travel around Timor-Leste dry open savannah vegetation to dense forest cover. Between the beaches and headlands, clumps of mangroves dot the coastlines, providing important fish breeding habitat.

Animals

With many centuries of habitation and subsistence living, Timor-Leste's larger native mammals and reptiles are reduced in number. That said, monkeys and spotted cuscus (a tree dwelling marsupial) live in the forests and there are rusa deer in the highlands. Reptiles include snakes, tokay lizards (one of the world's largest) and many other smaller geckos and skinks. Sea turtles come ashore to lay their eggs and estuarine crocodiles live in coastal habitats and Lake Ira Laloro. Bats and shrews are also seen.

Birdlife

Birdlife is more prolific and of vital interest to bird watchers. The strange mix of birds has Asian, Australian and Wallacean origins. Timor-Leste has over 240 species currently recorded, including 23 that are endemic, and more are being added with further research. The richness of Timor-Leste's birdlife, both resident and migrating, partly reflects the wide diversity of habitats, from mountain to coast and the country's geographic location. Timor-Leste still has relatively abundant numbers of some globally threatened species, including the yellow-crested cockatoo, black cuckoo dove, Timor sparrow and several other pigeon species.

Reefs & Ocean

TImor-Leste's fringing reefs are pristine and have extraordinary diversity. They lie within The Coral Triangle, which is recognised as the global epi-centre of marine biodiversity with regard to coral and fish species. Atauro, a small island lying to the north of Dili, has recently been found to have the most bio-diverse waters in the world in terms of reef fish. Researchers in a recent survey discovered a total of 642 species around the island and saw a maximum of 314 at a single site.

In Timor-Leste's clear tropical waters, divers and snorkellers are treated to an overwhelming display of reef fish, hard and soft corals and other species from nudi-branchs to sea horses, turtles to manta-rays, and if you are lucky dugongs and even whale sharks. Schooling open water fish species such as tuna, bonito and mackerel are also encountered. From vividly coloured coral 'bommies' in sheltered waters, to spectacular drop offs, Timor-Leste's marine life is some of, if not the best on the planet.

Whales & Dolphins

Timor-Leste is also regarded as a global hotspot for whales and dolphins due to their abundance, diversity and sheer density of numbers. They can be spotted year round and especially during the migration season, October to December. At that time Timor-Leste's deep waters become a major route between the Pacific and Indian Oceans for many different species.

Whale species include blue, killer, humpback, short-finned pilot, beaked, melon-headed and pigmy killer amongst others. Oceanic dolphins regularly seen include common, bottle-nosed, spinners, spotted, risso's, rough-toothed and striped. It is not uncommon during the migration to see whales and very large pods of dolphins both close in to the shore and from boats an exhilarating, unforgettable experience

People & Culture

The People
Timorese are fiercely proud of their independence and very aware of how hard they've had to fight for it. They are also quite stoic in the face of adversity, something honed through decades of tragedy. In many ways the population has been awakened to the possibilities ahead and that can explain some of the frequent internal upheavals. Without a common enemy in the form of the Indonesians, all manner of factions are vying for their place in the new East Timor. Old scores are being settled and spheres of power and influence calved out. People are not hesitant to protest perceived wrongs and this has led to frequent clashes in Dill and elsewhere, especially in old Fretilin strongholds.

Despite the chaotic images shown in news reports, the Timorese are one of the friendliest people you will encounter. Normally polite in a simple way you'll soon get hand fatigue from all the waving you'll be doing. Language issues aside, the Timorese are gregarious; in a nation this small, everybody seems to have one degree of separation.

There is a long collective memory, but the Portuguese from colonial are fading from consciousness, as are the Japanese from the war. It's much more complex regarding Indonesia: most adults in the country educated in Indonesian-run schools actually speak the language. And almost everybody had a loved one killed during the occupation, others married Indonesians sympathetic to the Timorese cause. Australia also poses a complex question. If any country could have stood for East Timor in 1975 but didn't it was Australia. Fretilin and others still resent perceived Australian meddling in local affairs, yet Australia's local importance, its leading role in trying to maintain peace from 1999 and the many Australians with a direct interest in, and friendship towards, East Timor make it a highly significant player.

Finally, many could learn lessons about stress reduction from the Timorese who don't expect things to work very well and are very adept at patiently adapting to the myriad challenges faced daily.

Culture

Because of the country's long period of colonization and diverse prehistoric ancestry, its culture is a reflection of a wide range of influences, from Malay to Portuguese, Austronesia, Catholic, and many indigenous tribes. Roman Catholicism has a very strong hold on the East Timorese, making the nation one of only three predominantly Catholic countries in Asia (the others being the Philippines and Armenia). Literature is also an important facet of the East Timorese cultural identity, as is weaving - a tradition still intact after generations.

Music is closely associated with the country's independence movement, as people used songs and anthems to build up the referendum. Aside from folk, East Timorese are also into pop music genres like hip hop, rock and roll and reggae. The Festival of Culture and Food of Timor Leste is an annual event that should not be missed.

Timorese customs
Hospitality is important to the East Timorese If you're offered food or drink when you meet somebody, it's important to at least taste it but always wait for your host to take the first sip or bite. As a result of the long Portuguese period, shaking hands is expected. Women often cheek or air kiss, usually on both sides of the face It's good form to greet others you pass on the street. And do as your mother always said: don't put your feet up on anything.

Always ask before taking photos or video of people but usually the East Timorese are quite happy to be photographed a sign that East Timor is not overrun with touristis. Say *"Bele?"* ("May I?" in Tetun) and you'll likely get a smiling *"bele,bele"* in response, which means "yes, yes", in contrast *"Labele"* would mean no and that the photo is not welcomed. East Timor is a conservative, largely traditional culture with strong Christian values. Elders, church and community leaders are treated with deference. As a general rule first names are only used among close acquaintances. Otherwise use "Senhor" (for men) or "Senhora" (for women).

Timorese Dance & Music
Bits of rock country, hip-flop, rap and even reggae can all be heard in East Timor's modern music. Guitars are popular and if there were garages there would be a lot of garage bands, especially in Dili. Instead you might say there are lots of under-trees bands across the country. No important East Timorese social gathering is complete without a band performing the types of cover songs that have been the staple of legions of globe-trotting Filipino bands to the north.

Usually a generator will be found for the synthesizer and the ballads can continue long into the night. Should you stumble upon a festival featuring traditional dancing and music, you are in for a rare treat. The *likurai* was primarily a Tetun dance used to welcome warriors returning from battle. Women danced with a small drum and circled the village compound where heads taken in battle were displayed. Today it is performed by unmarried women as a courtship dance. The *tebedai* dance is a circle dance performed throughout East Timor and it is accompanied by a drum.

Timorese Architecture
The traditional houses of East Timor vary from the large conical Bunak houses (*deuhoto*) in the west to the unique and iconic Fataluku houses in the east. The tall, elongated Fataluku houses have stilts supporting a main living room and are topped by a high, tapering thatched roof. A few have been built for display purposes, but you'll find many still in use on the road to Tutuala and in the region of Lantern and Lospalos. In Oecussi the hills are dotted with the traditional lopo and ume kebubu houses of the Dawan people, while all the way from Dill to the south coast you'll find the circular houses and conical roofs of the Mambat people. In Maliana, capital of the Bobonaro district and home to the Kemak people you'll see rectangular stilt houses.

Basket Weaving
Basket weaving is an important skill. Along the coast road between Dill and Manatuto village, craft workers hang their work out by the road to sell. Manatuto is also noted for its pottery work. On Atauro Island, directly north of Dill, a number of villages have their own distinct crafts, including wood carving and basket work. Arte Moris, an idiosyncratic and intriguing art school, gallery and social centre for a

new generation of Timorese artists. It's home to a growing number of artists in residence and is on the must do list for Dili.

Society

Timorese are incredibly hospitable, gregarious and some of the friendliest you'll ever encounter. Celebrations held at national and community levels are many and vibrant. Timorese society is also conservative and traditional with a strong focus on family, the community and religion.

Population

With a population of just over 1.1 million, Timorese are linked closely. At the same time many indigenous groups exist, each with its own language and cultural practices. Tetun is the largest of these accounting for approximately 25% of the population. They live around Dili, Suai and Viqueque. Mambae make up a further 10% and are found in the central mountains. Other groups include the Kemak, Bunak and Fataluku amongst others, each accounting for 5% or less.

Language

Timor-Leste (East Timor) has many spoken languages reflecting past migration, colonialism and other occupation. Tetun and Portuguese languages have been given official status, with Indonesian and English considered working languages. Another fifteen or more indigenous languages also are spoken.

Settlement

The capital of Dili is a modern developing city offering a wide range of services and amenities for residents and visitors. While many Timorese are drawn to the capital seeking employment, 70% still live in rural areas. These Timorese mostly reside in small towns and remote villages and practice a subsistence fishing and farming lifestyle.

Religion

Around 90% of Timorese identify as Roman Catholic and the remainder mostly as Protestant, Muslim and Hindu. In spite of this, animism continues to be a persuasive force in most peoples' everyday lives. Observing the way animist and religious beliefs are seamlessly blended is one of the interesting aspects of holidaying in this country.

Culture

Timorese cultural heritage is multi-layered a fascinating combination of traditional Timorese, Portuguese, Chinese and Indonesian influences. This permeates their local architecture, cuisine, clothing styles and artistic endeavors.

Timorese culture continues to evolve in local arts and handicrafts, as well as in dance and music. Cultural motifs, both old and modern, are incorporated into the design of tais hand-woven textiles, basket work and wood carving. Cultural groups still perform traditional dances and songs and also are entertaining in new ways. Talented Timorese bands and dance groups perform in local venues and at festivals.

Timor Leste Culture in more Detail

The island of Timor is very mountainous in relation to its size. The majestic mountains seem to rise without pattern that would be expected for ranges in other places. The river valleys cut into the mountains in most unlikely angles. They are always steep with fast running streams, especially when it rains. The total area of Timor is nearly 3,000 kilometres. It is one of the most easterly island in the Lesser Sunda archipelago, most of which belongs to Indonesia. East Timor has an area of about 19,000 square kilometres. For almost 450 years the area has been known as Portuguese Timor, but in 1976 was annexed by Indonesia as Timor Timur (East Timor), it's 27th province. In 1974, the last official Portuguese census, the population was 680,000. In 1980 the population was 555,350 according to the census conducted by the Indonesian authorities.

In Dili, the capital, it is always hot and there are only two seasons wet and dry.

The morals and social behaviour are not governed by our European standards, but it would be a mistake to regard the culture is in any way primitive. There is no doubt that much of its past culture has deprecated because of events that have occurred since 1975, nevertheless there will be enough of the old culture left to open the eyes of all who see it. It is important to look below the surface and the gain the most from your visit to the island. The KUTUAS (wise old men) say, "Only those with their eyes open can see."

Much of my own Timorese cultural knowledge may be historic, and not applicable to present day East Timor, though the fundamental beliefs of the Animists in Mother Earth must still exist in the minds of everyone in what is a very complicated culture. It is always hard to discover the deep intrinsic beliefs and mores of any society. I hope when you leave East Timor you will come away with some of the understanding and admiration I have for these very caring and brave people.

Timorese are of three different racial groups. But because of a long history of intertribal marriage there are no distinct physical features among people except in language. There are 16 languages and between 34 and 36 dialects. The people living along the south coast are Polynesian in language and custom, while those living on the north coast are Melanesian. In the mountains there are people who can be described by their language as Aboriginals.

Timor has had sophisticated contact with the world for many centuries. The Belu (Tetun) empire extended its power over much of the island but after the Europeans arrived much of the old empire contracted to its present area of indigenous Tetun speakers. The Chinese were regular visitors long before the Portuguese arrived in Timor. The indigenous lunar calendar is similar to the Chinese, the Timor pony has Asian origins and existed in Timor before the Portuguese. The musical instruments are Asian in design and sound.

It has been recorded in Chinese history that the Liurai at Besa Kama (the old Belu capital) paid a yearly tribute to China before the Portuguese Dominicans were on the scene in 1566. The attraction to Timor was because of its sandalwood, supposedly the best in the world. It was the sale of sandalwood that gave the Liurais their power and was the cause of their long past internecine wars. The Liurais wanted land - land that grew sandalwood, and with the land came people to harvest it. Sandalwood gave them the power to expand their empires. This greed of the Liurais caused their subjects to be involved in the danger of war. In the 16th and 17th centuries the Timorese had a reputation for being very warlike. The people of East Timor have a long long history of rebellion against their Portuguese colonial masters.

Timorese are by nature most polite with a great deal of outward humility and seem willing to agree to anything rather than upset strangers in their land. Thus it is easy to receive a wrong answer to questions, especially leading questions, merely because most people will only be trying to show good manners. Timorese respect others for their social position and education, as well as wealth, but they do not discriminate on the ground of race. This simple fact will put most Australians on an equal footing in their initial contact.

Timorese relatives cover a much wider circle than in Australia. Close kinship is regarded to exist among the uncles, aunts, and cousins of their in-laws' in-laws and a strong loyalty is given to all relatives. In past times the whole society revolved around incurring debts to ones relatives to build a bank of indebtedness for future help in all of the various tasks of living that could be accomplished more efficiently with a number of people, such as growing food, harvesting, house building, feasts, and the Animist religious ceremonies of death, birth and marriage.

Timorese culture was oral, therefore it is only natural that the people had developed strong skills in story telling and in poetry which could be told by anyone. But the ultimate in the art were the LIA NA'IN (also NA'I LIA, literally meaning lord of words), who could without hesitation relate verse on any subject at great length straight out of their heads. There were a number of traditional patterns, but the most common was DADOLIN, where each verse was in two lines and each line was in two phrases.

The first phrase of the second line repeated the meaning of the last phrase of the first verse but with different words. It was not uncommon for a skilled Lia Na'in to recite for hours, all of it verse that had never been heard until then. The actual words of the poetry rarely spoke on any subject with direct meanings. The true meanings were intended for people versed in the culture; e.g. reference to a blossom not yet in full bloom = a virgin; nectar tasted by many a girl of easy virtue; fruit eaten before it was ripe drought; things that move in the night spirits; dreaming of riches = greed; to cry alone loneliness, or deserted, and so on it went.

The real art was to repeat the important points as often as necessary to drive into the mind the message that the poet thought was needed. It is also important to keep in mind the Timorese philosophy that everything has a balancing opposite, such as hot and cold, wet and dry, good and bad, up and down, sky and earth, etc. which were also included in the poetry to complicate the telling.

In every village, the Katuas would tell stories to the children to instruct them in the lore and the code of behaviour of the clan so that on adulthood each person would know how to behave socially and know and accept their position in life. The society was very class conscious. Before the Portuguese the lowest class was LUTUN (the cattle keepers) then ATAN (slaves), EMA RAI (common people), DATO (nobility and royalty). Interspersed were MATAN DOOK (doctor), BUAN (sorcerer) MALULIK (keeper of sacred relics) and LIURAI (king). These were inherited upper class positions. From the Dato came ASU'UAIN (warriors). Marriage offered the only means of rising above the class into which one had been born.

A most important facet of Timorese life for Christians and non-Christians alike, was living with the KLAMAR (the souls of the dead) who had not gone to heaven or were unable to leave this earth for any reason. It was a Timorese belief that a wandering soul was always on the lookout to invade (or return to) the body of living persons where it would cause untold havoc and eventual death unless the klamar was persuaded to leave its new home. These spirits would enter the body through a number of body orifices.

Their favourite entry sites were the nose or eyes, never through the mouth or genital orifices. Not all spirits were evil. Some in fact were guardians to keep the evil ones away and in times of danger would appear to warn their ward so that a degree of stability continued to exist. Living in the Animist world was a continual struggle to keep life flowing with as much stability as possible. The MATAN DOOK (doctor) could invoke all sorts of potions (herbal medicine) and fetishes to nullify a HOROK (spell) from a klamar or one placed by the BUAN (sorcerer), who had very wide powers to create havoc among everyone.

His power was much stronger than the Matan Dook. The position of Matan Dook was handed on from father to son after many years of training. It was usually inherited among the Dato therefore it was a social status within the clan. The position of Buan could be inherited by any likely candidate with the proper aptitude after a long period of training and be either male or female, but usually male. A Buan had a religious standing in the community, which would give him a fearful respect. Even an important Liurai would treat a Buan with humble respect and fear. Within the orbit of the Animist religion all living things have souls, both plant and animal. Evil spirits came from creatures, especially those who spent the first half of their lives in water, and also came from the souls of people who lived a bad life.

Another being with supernatural power was the witch, in some areas known as KUKULASAK. In natural form she was an old woman, but had the power to transform herself into any other living thing. She could appear as a beautiful young woman to entice innocent people into sorts of danger with her beguiling ways. Every village had stories about witches appearing before some relative and by all sorts of trickery taking them away, never to be seen again. Some parents even told their children that witches like to eat people, especially plump, naughty children.

In the Animist religion it is believed that we are on this earth for a short period and after death on this earth we would return to the womb of the earth through the many vaginas that exist in the FATU KUAK (caves) in Timor. Therefore we must live a good life to return to our origins at the completion of the ephemeral stay on earth. All tribal debts have been repaid by our surviving relatives in order to free the soul and enable a feast to be held to celebrate the spirit's passage to heaven. Every community has a legend about the first men appearing out of the earth to form their clan. In previous times Timor was a cashless society and the wealth of an individual was assessed by the amount of livestock that they owned, such as horses, buffaloes, goats, pigs as well as gold and silver.

These animals were not used in everyday life as food. There was a much more important use for them; in life they showed how successful a person had been and in death many of these animals were slaughtered for the feast which sent the soul to heaven. Animals were NEVER sacrificed as a tribute to any religious ceremony, but as food for the invited guests. Feasts were held to celebrate births where the correct proportion of direct and in-law relatives were invited. As marriages were often arranged as political alliances rather than for any other reason, the guests at a birth feast could easily be from another kingdom far away. These feasts or gatherings served to reinforce obligations that each alliance placed on each clan and helped keep peace within the whole community.

At planting time special ceremonies were conducted to placate the Klamar and ensured that the guardian Klamar knew the seeds were being planted in the womb of Mother Earth. The guardian Klamar could then ensure the seeds were fruitful. If the planting was carried out at the first rain but no following rain occurred then it was said that an evil spirit had killed the soul of the plant and not that the farmer had made a mistake by planting too early. At harvest time it was always a race to reap the crops before the rats consumes the year's crop. Rats, of course, were the work of an evil spirit. The same was said if the plants became diseased, or failed for any other reason, like too much rain.

The UMA (house) in Timor was much more than a place for the family to live. In the Animist religion there was no church, and the family home served this purpose much better. The traditional house had two poles as its base foundation. These two poles represented the male and female (all things in Timor came in pairs), and divided the house into two areas, where the woman of the house ruled supreme. Because the house had this religious significance. The woman of the house acted as the religious head of the family. On the female pole hung the woven bags containing the dried placentas of the occupants of the house. These articles should follow each person throughout their life, otherwise they had no protection against any Klamar. Also each person would not be able to return to Mother Earth as whole person on their death.

Disasters were accepted with stoic fatalism as the work of an evil spirit. Even accidents were ascribed to fetishes or invasions of spirits. Therefore the Timorese were able to accept the most horrific ill-fortune and still be able to carry on as if nothing out of the ordinary had happened. Because of the importance of combating the effects of the Klamar, some people would change their name after a serious misfortune so that the Klamar would not know them any more, and nothing would persuade them to admit to being previously known by their prior name, which was very disconcerting for the Portuguese conducting the biannual census. During the Second World War the Australian soldiers in East Timor employed many adolescent boys to help them with their baggage.

One day while being chased by the Japanese, we had to cross a flooded stream. The usual method was to enter the stream with the upstream leg bent and down stream leg stiff and by a forward hopping action progress across to the other bank. During the course of crossing two of the Timorese boys were hit by rocks along along the bed of the stream and were swept down stream and drowned. The Australian soldiers were most upset with such a tragic personal loss but the Timorese said, "We are here to protect the Australians. All the Australians are safe, and that is all that is important." It would have been very bad manners to have shown grief to us. There are many other instances that could be related about the care for other people the Timorese showed us during our war in Timor.

Marriage and the arrangement of marriage consumed a great deal of time and ceremony. The usual and preferred method was by HAFOLI (lit:to fix the value) where a go-between (a katuas close to the family) would spend up to a year and even longer fixing the terms of the alliance. The proper gifts were passed to each side as the terms were gradually sorted out. At each stage the Lia Na'in would recite long lengths of poetry DADOLIN (two line verse) emphasising the merits of the alliance to the opposite side.

A Lia Na'in from the other side would do the same, as the guests ate food supplied by the groom's relatives. When the terms had been agreed upon, and the initial gifts exchanged, (buffalo, and horses from the groom's family as well as gold and silver, and from the bride's family goats, pigs and cloth) the two young people often lived together on a nightly basis in the house of the girl's parents. Consummation was the only recognised rite of marriage. Now that so many Timorese are Christian, the priests could be insisting on a marriage ceremony similar to that conducted in our churches.

In times past marriage was not entered upon lightly. Firstly the prospective groom would approach his parents for permission to marry. Then the elders would decide if the young man was a suitable candidate to become a full member of the clan, as only married men and women were allowed to enter fully into all the religious rites and secrets. If for any reason the elders decided that the young man was not suitable to become a full clan member (as a practising priest of Mother Earth), then no arrangement could be made for his marriage.

Of course this does not happen any more. Since 1975 many young men take the woman of their choice as their wife without any ceremony. This is called HAFE. Unlike in our Western culture, marriage between first cousins is not frowned upon, provided the nuptial couple were the children of a brother or sister. Two children of sisters or brothers was strictly forbidden.

Slavery was an accepted way of life even in 1975. It was a very benign practice, but it still existed, even though it had been outlawed by the Portuguese. It was not uncommon for young boys and some girls to be sold into slavery. I personally know some young Timorese refugees who were slaves in Timor. Another way of describing the practice would be to say the ATAN (slave) was an unpaid servant, also called KREADO (nurse for a baby), who was not free to leave the family. Their masters were responsible for their welfare and usually the slave was treated humanely. It was not unusual for a slave to become part of the family to such a degree that on adulthood he married a daughter of the family.

The Timorese have a special reverence for death. It was the time when the virtues of the deceased were told to the world at great length by the mourners. The demise of an important clan member meant much displacement of power, with new positions to be filled. Sometimes it was found that the only solution was to offer the position to someone in a neighbouring clan.

n extreme situations the clan was split into two. It has been said to me by a KATUAS (wise old man) that by nature man is a spiller of blood, and is incapable of controlling his actions which are against the needs of Mother Earth, where harmony will ensure a fruitful life for humans. Therefore it is better for him to satisfy his instinct outside his family, so that he can live in harmony at home with his wife and children.

After about a year, all the relatives and those who had a debt owing to them, or those who had an alliance with the deceased were invited to a KORE METAN (celebration of departure) back to where the soul of the deceased had emerged form the womb of Mother Earth. Many final debts were repaid in the work involved in the preparation of the feast. The guests gorged themselves with meat and TUAKA (palm wine) for anything up to a week of dancing and telling stories of the virtues of the departed.

I do not purport that what has been written is anything but a thumbnail sketch of the psyche of East Timorese culture, because it is difficult to obtain more than a glimpse into the religious life of the

Timorese Animist world. I am happy if it helps the traveller have a greater understanding and appreciation of life in East Timor.

Perspectives

Cultural Information - Conversations
Question:
I am meeting someone for the first time and I want to make a good impression. What would be good discussion topics?

Local Perspective:
East Timor or Timor-Leste is a tiny country that takes up half of Timor Island and has about 800 000 people. It has almost 16 different ethnic groups and 32 dialects. Major ethnic groups are divided according to the number of dialect speakers, which are Mambae, Tetun or Fehan, Makasae, Fataluku, Bunak, Kemak and Atoni.

Indigenous culture which is practised by Timorese is largely influenced their traditional animist beliefs. East Timor or Timor-Leste culture had also suffered from exterior influences. The country had been famous in the past for its sandalwood and had been communicating with other traders such as Indians and Chinese prior to the arrivals of the Portuguese. Traders had been the first outsiders that brought new components to Timorese culture. Portuguese culture, after 400 years of colonization has also had a large influence on Timorese culture.

Finally, 24 years of being Indonesia's 27thprovince has brought new components to the culture.

It is common for Timorese to shake hands when meeting a stranger for the first time. While shaking hands, Timorese look the stranger in the eyes briefly and flash a smile to show their high respect to the stranger. Introduction of names, and talking about the district or country one is from can be done at this time. Or one can also greet the stranger with, "How are you" when shaking hands.

After this stage, usually Timorese proceed to other general topics of conversation. Usually Timorese keep brief and continuous eye contact with the person they are speaking to and still flash out a brief smile. This shows respect and consideration to the person one is talking to.

Cultural Information - Communication Styles
Question :
What do I need to know about verbal and non-verbal communications?

Local Perspective:
Touching the person that you meet for the first time is not common and you would always keep distance when speaking. In your conversation, it is not common also to ask if the other person is married, how many kids he or she has or who are his/her parents. If

your tone of voice during the conversation is too loud people will feel offended.

Cultural Information - Display of Emotion
Question:
Are public displays of affection, anger or other emotions acceptable?

Local Perspective:
Public displays of affection or anger are not acceptable and not common in East Timor, or Timor-Leste. Expressing anger publicly is considered rude and insulting to the person he/she is addressing and will harm future meetings.

Women may kiss each other in public even if they are only meeting for the first time. Men will only shake hands with women when meeting them for the first time and vice-versa. Only men and women that have a close family relationship kiss each other in public.

It is considered taboo for non-legally-married couples to kiss or hug each other publicly.

Cultural Information - Dress, Punctuality & Formality
Question:
What should I know about the workplace environment (deadlines, dress, formality, etc.)?

Local Perspective:

Dress for work is quite modest in Timor-Leste because of tropical weather. For women, a skirt and blouse or a long dress are acceptable. For men, long trousers and long or short sleeved shirts are common dress. For very formal occasions, suites are required.

In the work place, Timorese address their colleagues with " Senhor A" and Senhora B", which literally mean Mr. and Mrs, regardless of his/her level.

Timorese approach to time is quite relaxed. People are use to arriving to the office or to appointments or meetings late.

Living in an extended family style, Timorese feel related to everybody, which makes them always have an excuse to leave the office at working hours and to go for familiar occasions ceremonies.

Due to the lack of local human resources, productivity at workplaces is low and people wait to be told to carry out their jobs.

Cultural Information - Preferred Managerial Qualities
Question:
What qualities are most highly regarded in a local superior/manager?
How will I know how my staff view me?

Local Perspective:
Apart from having education, experience and leadership qualities, a local or expat superior or manager should be hard working and

disciplined in whatever relates to the job in order to be an example for other colleagues. Being personable is another quality required for a manager in terms of his/her interaction with other colleagues. A manager should avoid showing an attitude of superiority because it will hinder him/her in leading his/her colleagues and managing the office.

It is common for Timorese to talk about their manager with each other when they feel unhappy with him/her. They will usually not show to their manager his/her weaknesses directly. The only way to get their views on you is through friendly and one-one dialogue.

Cultural Information - Hierarchy and Decision-making

Question:
In the workplace, how are decisions taken and by whom? Is it acceptable to go to my immediate supervisor for answers or feedback?

Local Perspective:
The top-down management style, which is still common in Timor-Leste means that all the decisions are taken by the manager or leader. However, a manager may consult his/her colleagues prior to taking the decision.

Ideas are generated mainly by the manager, although sometimes with a small group.

It is acceptable to go to one's supervisor for answer and feedback.

Cultural Information - Religion, Class, Ethnicity, & Gender

Question:
Briefly describe the local culture's attitudes regarding the following: Gender, Class, Religion and Ethnicity. What impact would the above attitudes have on the workplace?

Local Perspective:
Gender: Gender is a new way of thinking in Timor-Leste. Timor Leste has a paternalistic style in which women play the role of housewife, look after the kids and cook. Men, on the other hand, are responsible for earning the money to support the family and are the ones who are involved in community's decisions and activities. However men have high respect towards women and they are very protective of women in case of women are in trouble.

One should be careful interacting with a colleague' girl-/boyfriend or spouse (if you are the opposite sex). Timorese are very protective in this sense and they can react very strongly if they feel threatened.

Religion: Prior to Portuguese arrival in the island 400 years ago, animism was as the dominant religion of the Timorese. Portuguese missionaries introduced Christianity to the island and now, 90 percent of Timorese are Catholic and roughly 70 percent are observant.

Protestants are the second major religion in Timor-Leste, after which come Animism and Islam. Catholic church hierarchy has big power to influence the socio and political life of Timorese because of its long tradition of interaction with the people, at all levels of communities and government. Any sensible thought, practice or ideas against Catholicism and its teachings could eventually create serious social problems because of reactions from fanatic believers.

Class: In some parts of the countryside there are two classes of people. First, is the family of the leader of the community and second, all other members of the community.

Ethnicity: In the workplace one should use common sense in the interaction with other colleagues and avoid sensitive issues regarding religion and ethnicity. Conflicts between ethnic groups are common in Timor-Leste and often start because somebody insults or minimizes or puts down a person from another ethnic group. When this occurs, the conflict usually ends up being a group conflict and can be quite dangerous.

Cultural Information - Relationship-building
Question:
How important is it to establish a personal relationship with a colleague or client before getting to business?

Local Perspective:
Personal relationships with colleagues or clients is really important in terms of decreasing the feeling of distance, making them feel please and comfortable and to feel that workplace is like their home. Start your relationship with light topics of common interest before getting to your real business. You can also give him/her small presents of some value from your region or visit his/her house, family as part of starting a relationship.

When Timorese host a visitor they do not ask him or her what to drink and eat, they just offer whatever they see as a best offer. Rejecting the offer is considering an offence to the person that makes the offer.

In the community or in the workplace one should continuously take the initiative to greet or say hello to everybody in order to deepen one's interaction and relation with others. In your work break time try to set aside time to chat with whomever, regardless of his or her rank.

Cultural Information - Privileges and Favoritism
Question:
Would a colleague or employee expect special privileges or considerations given our personal relationship or friendship

Local Perspective:
There is a mentality inherited from Indonesian regime's occupation of colleagues or employees expecting privileges or considerations

because of their relationship or friendship. Examples of the preferential treatment they would expect would be in the application of office rules and disciplines, or the hiring his/her friends or family members if there is a vacancy open at your work place. This type of practice is socially rejected and when somebody comes across the situation, he or she should politely approach his or her colleague/employee to explain the reasons for not agreeing to such practices.

Cultural Information - Conflicts in the Workplace

Question:
I have a work-related problem with a colleague. Do I confront him or her directly? Privately or publicly?

Local Perspective:
If you have a work-related problem with a colleague at your workplace, you should not confront him or her in public directly. Approach him or her softly and have a private conversation without making early judgement against him or her. Ask his/her views on what how you see the situation and then (if you are the manager) try politely to show him/her where his/her strengths and weaknesses are and suggest ways for future improvements.

If somebody is having problems with you or is offended by something you have done, he/she will always avoid looking at you or speaking to you. If he/she walks in your direction and does not greet or flash a smile at you; that is a sign. It is easy to read from Timorese faces when they feel annoyed with somebody.

Cultural Information - Motivating Local Colleagues
Question:
What motivates my local colleagues to perform well on the job?

Local Perspective:
Your local colleagues will feel motivated when you express that you are pleased with their work and they will, in turn, feel proud of themselves and have more confidence to perform the job in the future.

Timorese have a strong commitment to carry out any job as long as they have the knowledge and skills on it. Due to the lack of capacity building opportunities in Timor-Leste, training a person to perform a job well is really necessary.

Money is one of the major motivations for Timorese. As a manager you should ensure that the salary payment is done precisely on time. Any delay of payment will productivity at work.

Good working condition in terms of physical and psychological environment are needed and will make Timorese feel at home in the workplace.

Cultural Information - Recommended Books, Films & Foods

Question:
To help me learn more about the local culture(s), please recommend: books, films, television shows, foods and web sites.

Local Perspective:
Timor-Leste is a nation of one and a half years old, making access to books, film, Television shows, Websites to visits, news papers, TV/radio sporting events, and comedy shows difficult. However, information can be gathered from Canadians such as RCMP police members that were deployed for one or two years in the country, or through Canadian Civil Society organizations e.g. CARE Canada, CUSO and USC officers.

Cultural Information - In-country Activities

Question:
When in this country, I want to learn more about the culture(s) and people. What activities can you recommend?

Local Perspective:
Timor-Leste has great potential for tourism. One can enjoy the warm weather of costal areas or easily reach the upland sites for a fresh or colder climate. The eastern part of the country is famous for its crocodiles and Tutuala and the island of Jaco are interesting sites to visit. Mount of Ramelau, the highest mountain of the country, located

in the central part, is another good place to visit. Atauro, the island opposite the capital Dili, is an interesting site to visit.

Frequent individual contacts with either local Timorese or Expats that have stayed long in the country could be potential sources for cultural interpreters.

In terms of food, there are Portuguese, Asian and traditional dishes served in restaurants in the urban sites.

Travel and Tourism
Things to Do

Things to do in East Timor usually involve the outdoors. At 2,986 m, Mount Ramelau attracts recreational climbers. Around the mountain are challenging treks and bike trails. Nino Konis National Park is also worth visiting. This eco park can be found in the east of the country and is a one-stop shop for bird-watching, trekking, diving and prehistoric archeological sites.

From the depths off the coast of Tibar to the islands of Atauro and Jaco, East Timor is known for its fabulous dive sites, especially and the ever-popular Dili Rock. Marvel at the beauty of the region's marine life or laze around the breathtaking Areia Branca Beach or the sunny Cape Fatucama. Other sites to check out are East from Dili, Dili and West, and Lospalos.

The longest running dive operator in the center in the country is *FreeFlow Diving*. It is also the first PADI resort in East Timor, teaching and training beginners and professionals. It is one of two major dive companies, the other being *Dive Timor-Lorosae*, which specializes in boat charters, whale watching, diving, and fishing tours.

Sightseeing and adventure packages around East Timor are available through *Grand Touring*, an established travel company offering one- to five-day tours. Hiking to the top of Ramelau or climbing the equally breathtaking Mount Matebian is one of the itinerary highlights. Those who want a more relaxed day can join a coffee tour of the beautifully landscaped coffee growing fields. The town of Aileu is also worth checking out for its historic buildings, including the church and the iconic Falintil training camp.

Eco Discovery offers some of the best tour packages around the country, ranging from guided tours of the capital city of Dili to trekking expeditions, safaris, bird watching, and scenic drives to some of the most remote locations in the region. Those looking for culture can gain insight into the history and local customs of the Timorese via *Timor Sparrow Force Tours*.

Timor Leste is home to one of the most arduous bike races in the world (Tour de Timor), but for non-athletes, there are many scenic and relaxing cycling trails to discover too, especially around the rugged Oecussi. However, beginners should beware of the steep and often tricky, mostly unpaved bike paths. *Compass Charters & Ocean Adventures* offers adventure packages that including mountain biking and guide-led dives.

Week-long trips around Timor-Leste are best organized by *Intrepid*, who specializes in sightseeing and shopping tours around the markets of Dili, cross-island trips and even historic tours of Venilale's war hideouts. Volunteer projects are continuously underway around the country, and visitors are more than welcome to participate in enriching and rewarding community building. Below are some of activities and attractions.

Arts & Crafts

Timorese are very creative with their unique style and workmanship.

Their most famous handicrafts are tais (traditional hand woven fabrics), many of which are sought by serious collectors. Tais are produced in different colours and designs depending on the community where they are made.

Other attractive arts and handicrafts include finely woven baskets and mats, paintings, pottery, jewelry, dolls and intricately embroidered bags, musical instruments, metal knives and wood carvings.

Locally purchased arts and crafts make a wonderful gift and can be readily sourced from handicraft shops, roadside stalls and at local markets throughout Timor-Leste. One of the joys of travelling in the districts is when you come across local people creating beautiful items such as weaving cane ware, working a back-strap loom or carving figurines

Beaches

Timor-Leste has many stunning beaches, from the more popular such as Areia Branca and Back Beach near Dili to those almost deserted. You'll love them. For your beach experience drive out along the coast from Dili or take a boat trip to Atauro.

They include pristine tropical paradises along the northern coast such as the white sand beaches to the east near Baucau, on both sides of Com, at Valu and around exquisite Jaco Island. Beautiful silver-grey beaches lie to the west.

Atauro Island also has some untouched gems around its coastline which are perfect for beach walking and relaxation.

In Timor-Leste water temperatures are warm all year round and clarity is very high making swimming irresistible.

Sunrise and sunset are special times and the colours reflecting on the water are often mesmerising

Birding

Of vital interest to bird watchers is Timor-Leste's bio-geographically mixed bird life (Asian and Australian). There are more than 240 bird species, including at least 23 found nowhere else in the world. The very high diversity of bird species reflects Timor-Leste's extremely wide range of habitats and geographic location.

These unique bird species include relatively abundant numbers of the globally threatened Timor green pigeon, Timor imperial pigeon, yellow crested cockatoo, black cuckoo dove and the Timor sparrow.

Come and be surprised.

Diving

Located within the famous Coral Triangle, Timor-Leste has some of the most pristine, ecologically diverse and least explored dive sites on the globe. The marine life is abundant with colourful hard and soft corals as well as a vivid array of reef fish.

Open water species such as tuna and mackerel are encountered along with harmless reef and whale sharks, manta rays, turtles and the more elusive dugongs.

In more sheltered sites you'll marvel at the variety of fascinating smaller critters displaying weird and wonderful shapes and colours.

Reefs run close to the shore along much of Timor-Leste's northern coast, immediately in front of the capital Dili and around Atauro and Jaco Islands. Sites range from more sheltered and gently sloping fringing reefs to magnificent wall diving with underwater cliffs plunging into the abyss.

Most of the best dive sites are very accessible some requiring just a short swim from the beach.

Warm tropical waters provide excellent visibility all year around.

The availability of experienced diving companies makes Timor-Leste an epic dive location whether you are a novice or veteran. Local diving companies provide shore and boat dives, PADI courses and overnight dive safaris. Shore dives are offered in close proximity to Dili, at dive sites to the west and east along the northern coast.

Atauro Island is another very popular destination for guided diving adventures from Dili and all companies run their own boats. Atauro

Dive Resort is located at Beloi on Atauro and Compass Charters has a beach house at Beloi and diving eco-camp at Adara.

Coffee

If you are a coffee drinker you are in for a treat when you holiday in Timor-Leste. Coffee produced here is high quality, delicious and exported all over the world. It is a hot commodity selling at a premium price on the global market with main markets United States, Germany, Portugal, Indonesia and Australia. The Timorese are also great coffee drinkers, with a preference for it black and very strong.

Coffee has been organically grown for over 200 years in Timor-Leste's steep highlands and the coffee forests with their large shade tree canopies now cover an estimated 52,000 ha.

It is the country's biggest agricultural export and employer with over 50,000 Timorese families relying on the coffee harvest for a substantial part of their income. Both arabica and robusta varieties are grown plus the arabica-robusta hybrid which miraculously provides in a single plant the best qualities of both species. These are well suited to Timor-Leste's natural conditions and climate.

During the main harvest, June to August, you'll see the Timorese picking the red coffee cherries and if travelling in the producing areas you'll need to veer around patches drying in the sunshine on the road edge. Ermera accounts for half of Timor-Leste's coffee production with other important areas being Ainaro, Aileu, Manufahi, Liquica and Bobonaro.

Dolphins & Whales

Viewing dolphins and whales in the wild is totally exhilarating and Timor-Leste is a top location for this.

While dolphins and especially the smaller whales, such as short-finned pilot and melon-headed, can be seen year round, from October to December the Wetar Strait separating Dili and Atauro becomes a major migratory route (a marine super highway) between the Pacific and Indian Oceans. During this time different species of whales, from massive to smaller, including the blue, beaked, humpback, sperm, killer, short-finned pilot and melon-headed, along with very large pods of dolphins can be viewed from cruise boats and the shoreline.

Marine scientists refer to Timor-Leste as a global hotspot for whales and dolphins due to their abundance, diversity and sheer density of numbers.

Some of the diving operators run dolphin & whale watching cruises on a charter basis during the migration season.

Eating & Drinking

Timor-Leste has a strong culture of hospitality and most socialising involves food.

A traditional Timorese lunch or dinner meal includes rice, meat or fish, beans and corn, seasonal vegetables with clever use of local spices, fresh herbs, tropical fruits and sometimes coconut milk accompanied by extremely hot ai-manis (chili paste).

Timor-Leste is rightly famous for its rich, dark and delicious coffee, grown organically in the hills. As you explore Timor-Leste it is interesting sampling the different coffee. Bags of freshly roasted coffee beans make a great gift to take home.

For a city of its size, Dili has a wide range of restaurants reflecting many differing influences. International options include Chinese, Portuguese, Indian, Thai, Turkish, Italian, Japanese, Korean, Indonesian and Brazilian, amongst others. These vary from the up market to the very casual. Many have beautiful views out over the water where you can enjoy the sunset. Daily caught seafood and organically grown fruit and vegetables from local farmers influence their menus. Most restaurants serve beer and wine, and a few pour an excellent cocktail.

There are also dedicated bars, some of which have local Timor-Leste bands.

Small bakeries and cafes in Dili are other popular meeting places.

In the evenings food stalls grill fresh seafood along the beachfront and this can be enjoyed with a cold drink as you take in the views.

Out in the districts larger guesthouses usually provide meals in-house and there are other small restaurants mostly 'warung' style. Along the coastal roads grilled fish stalls also are readily available.

Fishing

The ocean around Timor-Leste provides excellent fishing opportunities. Local people are adept with net, spear and trap. Arrange to go out with Timorese fishers in their colourful wooden craft for inshore fishing or charter a larger tourism boat and head for the deep.

Potential big game fish that ply Timorese waters include giant trevally, yellow fin tuna, Spanish mackerel, sailfish and marlin.

One of the joys of travelling in Timor-Leste definitely is eating freshly caught barbecued fish (with a squeeze of fresh lime juice).

Events & Festival

There is vibrancy and youthfulness about Timor-Leste. This is definitely part of its charm which most who visit find very refreshing. Timorese in general are gregarious and they like to party. Usually that means joining together with family, friends and neighbours, sharing food and drink, music, dancing and often fireworks. If passing by you are likely to be asked to join in.

At the national level, in addition to important religious holidays such as All Souls, All Saints, Christmas and Easter, most other holidays celebrate Timor-Leste's recent independence as a nation. Popular Consultation, Restoration of Independence, Proclamation of Independence and National Youth Days are examples. Participating in these special Timor-Leste commemorations is a great way to learn more about this nation and to meet its people.

Then there are the cultural events, such as music festivals, and international sporting events designed to foster national unity and showcase the warmth and beauty of Timor-Leste.

The most famous of these are the Dili 'City of Peace' Marathon and one of the world's toughest bike races the grueling Tour de Timor. Its 400-500km route varies from year to year and whether you are one of the hardy participants or a bystander it is inspiring.

Heritage & Culture

As a newly independent country and still largely off the beaten path, Timor-Leste is a fascinating place to visit both in terms of heritage and culture, and its general way of life.

Timor-Leste culture is strong, unique and reflects many different influences: traditional animist beliefs; a former Portuguese colony; the impact of WWII; the more recent Indonesian invasion and spirited Timorese resistance; the role of the Catholic Church and the effects of other minority groups such as Chinese traders.

Do visit the excellent Timorese Resistance Archive and Museum in Dili if you are interested in learning more about the struggle independence.

Timor-Leste's traditional music, dance and story-telling is a fundamental part of its cultural heritage and very engaging to watch. So definitely make the most of any opportunities, whether a small local occasion or a national fiesta.

There is much of interest for travelers in Timor-Leste. In addition to main attractions and learning about significant historical events, it is fun to wander around a local market or back street and experience everyday life. Timorese are extremely hospitable and proud of their country and if you express an interest and openness, they are happy to share information and on occasion their personal stories.

Hiking & Walking

Timor-Leste is made for hiking with stunning scenery, friendly locals and a network of tracks criss-crossing the entire country. From coastal walks to multi-day village and mountain hikes, Timor-Leste has some excellent options.

Even close to Dili there is fantastic walking, including the 'Horta Loop' a 2-3 hours circuit from Areia Branca which includes Back Beach and coastal views from the Cristo Rei statue a top Cape Fatucama.

From Hato Builico, the three hours guided walking ascent of Mt Ramelau, Timor-Leste's highest mountain, is a must. Watching the sun rise over Timor-Leste from the summit is a sight not to be missed. In the surrounding hills there are also other great hikes to remote villages and sacred sites.

Towards the eastern end of the island, Mt Matebian and the lost world of Mundo Perdido are popular ascents, although much more demanding. To the south is Mt Kablaki in Same district. Other well-known areas for hiking are Lautem, Oecusse, Maliana and Atauro, which have treks ranging from coastal to rugged mountain.

Tourism operators in Dili can prearrange some fantastic multi-day walking adventures with transport, accommodation, food and guides or alternatively, on arrival in the districts, trekking guides can be organised by enquiring at the main guest houses.

Hiring a hiking guide is a necessity as they know the terrain, hazards, cultural sensitivities and language. You are likely to find out more about the local area and it's a great way of helping put some money into the community

Local Markets

To gain an insight into Timorese communities and daily life wander around the markets. They are lively, interesting places with local seasonal produce, handicrafts and other goods on display.

They are a great place to meet the local people and of course to stock up on fresh fruit and vegetables, snacks and other items.

In larger centres, markets are held daily, but in smaller towns they are a weekly highlight with people travelling long distances on foot, horseback, small boat, truck and motorcycle from surrounding villages

Mountain Biking

Timor-Leste's compact size, scenic diversity and relatively light traffic mean mountain biking is an interesting and fun way to explore the country. That said, if you head inland, hills are extremely rugged and some of the steeper sections are brutal. Mountain biking in Timor-Leste is definitely not for the faint hearted.

While a few places hire bikes in Dili and on Atauro for day use, basic bikes can be purchased in Dili for around USD300. If you are an enthusiast, it is definitely recommended you bring your own gear.

Each year one of the world's toughest mountain bike races is held the gruelling Tour de Timor

Surfing, Diving and Snorkeling

Timor-Leste's diving is not only spectacular but also very accessible. The bulk of the regularly visited dive sites are located either in Dili or near Maubara in the west. The drive out to the sites to the east of Dili is part of the adventure, as you rise above the sea before descending to the dive sites. All of these sites can be accessed from the shore. Drive up to the beach, unload in the shade, gear up and walk into the water.

Within minutes, schools of fish, colorful corals, marine critters and dugongs surround you. The diving is not deep either, so more time is spent seeing marine activity rather than decompressing. Boat dives can get access to the sites in and around Dili, in addition to the underwater paradise of Atauro Island. If you can get a group of six or eight divers together, these boat dives are similarly priced to those from the shore. Further along the east coast, the Dili dive operators can arrange dive safaris to sites around Corn, Tutuala and Jam Island.

This can be done by vehicle or boat, or you can go by car and meet the boat there. The expense increases for these trips, but the dive sites are well worth the effort for their rich coral and sea life. Those who want to learn to dive in East Timor will find a full suite of PADI courses on offer in Dili. Courses start at $255 (US dollars) and include dives at some of the Country's best sites. Discuss your requirements with the dive operators who will be able to put together a package that will cater for your needs and budget.

Snorkeling Timor-Leste

Everyone that comes to Timor-Leste (East Timor) should go snorkeling. A mask and a snorkel is every season's must-have accessory. It is always good to bring your own mask and snorkel equipment with you. Although dive operators cam supply them. a well-fitting mask is essential and it also means you can go snorkeling at any time!

There are two ways you are going to be able to do some snorkeling: either under your own steam or with a dive operator. Going independent is easy, particularly if you have a vehicle. As the reef hugs the north coast, pulling over on one of the deserted beaches for a look can prove to be an underwater paradise. There is also good snorkeling to be had at the existing dive sites. Ask around where you are staying, as most people are happy to share their favorite spots with you. Just like with diving, keep your buddy close and be careful of currents.

One of the great things about diving in East timor is that with the prevalence of shore diving, your non-diving friends and family can easily join you. Add operators are comfortable taking non-divers on the trips to the dive sites for a reduced fee. Snorkelers can still have amazing experience, as a lot of the coral and marine life is also accessible to them.

Planning Your Diving & Snorkeling Trip

Diving is possible year-round, although the conditions are smoother and the water clearer during the May to November dry sea-son when visibility is typically 20m to 30m. During the wet season, from December to April, the visibility is still 15m to 20m. February is probably the worst month for visibility with some sites affected, to varying degrees, by silt run-off from the swollen rivers comping from the torrential downpours. It picks up again by mid- to late March, and in April visibility is once again excellent. September is great for manta rays and, if you are lucky whale sharks. Some dive sites can experience strong currents and are more suitable for advanced, experienced divers. The water temperatures fluctuates between 26°C and 28°C year-round.

Why is the Diving So Good?
The diving in Timor-Leste (East Timor) is world class, thanks to a perfect mix of cool, deep water, undamaged reefs, under fished marine life and its prime location in the Coral Triangle. Ocean trenches that reach several kilometers deep yield cool thermo climes that rejuvenate the coral life, which is also relatively untouched compared with East Timor's neighbors, such as Indonesia and the Philippines. The practice of dynamite fishing never caught on because explosives were so tightly controlled during the Indonesian occupation.

The sea life is as plentiful as it is diverse, from nudibranchs to turtles to schooling trivially. Scientists travel halfway around the world to see one or two of the species of fish or sponge that are so plentiful in East Timor. Large-scale commercial fishing has not started around any of the dive sites, and supplies are now in equilibrium with what the locals eat and sell to foreigners in Dili 's restaurants.

This perfect mix treats divers to a colorful array of hard and soft corals as well as a vivid assortment of reef fish. Pelagics (open-water species such as tuna, bonito and mackerel) are regularly encountered, along with harmless reef sharks, manta rays, dolphins and dugongs. The coral reef runs close to the shore along much of the north coast, and divers have only to wade in and swim a few strokes to reach spectacular drop-offs.

The Coral Triangle

Timor-Leste (East Timor) lies in the southwest corner of the pristine Coral Triangle, which also includes the tropical marine waters of Indonesia, Malaysia, the Philippines, Papua New Guinea and the Solon-ion Islands. Scientists believe that each eco-region contains at least 500 species of reef-building corals. The Triangle encompasses portions of two biographic regions: the Indonesian-Philippines Region (where East Timor lies) and the Far Southwestern Pacific Region. The Coral Triangle is recognized as the global epicenter of marine biodiversity and has the highest coral diversity in the world, with 76% of the world's 805 coral species found there. Moreover, 37% of the world's coral-reef fish can also be found in the Triangle, which is the highest diversity of coral-reef fish in the world.

Surfing Timor-Leste

More recently we have watched the emergence of the practice of Surfing in Timor-Leste. If you are a surf practitioner don't forget to visit the resources that this island has to offer

National Park

In 2007, the Government of Timor-Leste declared its first national park, Nino Konis Santana National Park. This national park includes the entire eastern tip of Timor-Leste and the waters off shore. It was named after the commander of the Falantil who was born locally in Tutuala and died in 1998.

Covering 123,600ha from forested mountain ranges to a marine area with magnificent coral reefs, the park also includes Lake Ira Lalaro and Jaco Island. The adjoining reef system is part of the globally significant 'Coral Triangle' having extremely high diversity of reef fish and coral species.

The dense forest within the park includes both tropical lowland vine forest thick with orchids and ferns, as well as monsoon forest with banyan, rosewood and fig trees. Rusa deer, cuscus, monkeys, over 200 species of birds and five species of sea turtles are resident wildlife.

Furthermore, this national park's designation is of enormous cultural significance with many sacred sites located within the boundary. Limestone caves, some with ancient rock art are good examples.

While the Nino Konis Santana National Park is still in the process of being established in terms of facilities and enforced protections its designation is an important step in the on-going conservation of this beautiful and environmentally important area.

Attractions

Most of the attractions in East Timor involve the sea and the coast, but the capital city and surround area also offer a picturesque vacation backdrop. The colonial times have left traces of history, from gutted buildings to remarkable structures, especially in the capital of Dili, which also serves as the country's main economic hub. The best way to explore the country is on a guided tour, but if you are feeling adventurous, rent a car and go at it on your own. You can also explore Dili by taxi and mikrolet or take a bus between towns.

Resistance Museum
Established early in 2012, this young museum commemorates East Timor's 24-year resistance against the Indonesian reign. It opened in the wake of the country's 10th anniversary of independence and features exhibitions, photographs, equipment, and other items related to the revolution. Address: Rua Formosa Central Dili, behind the National Parliament and next to the university

Jesus Statue
Standing tall over Cape Fatucama is a 27-meter statue of Jesus, one of the most iconic monuments in East Timor. While here, be sure to

make the scenic trip along the inspiring coastal road. Taxis can take you from town to the coast for next to nothing, but you have to pay extra if you want the driver to wait while you explore. Address: Cape Fatucama

Arte Moris
Arte Moris is an art institution and museum set in an Indonesian-era building. It features interesting works from the whimsical to the wonderful. Art lovers will appreciate the funky and hip sculpture garden and many impressive masterpieces in the gallery. Address: Rua Martires da Patria Comoro Phone: +670-331-0346 Website: http://www.artemoris.org/

Santa Cruz Cemetery
A monument commemorating the turning point in the Timorese independence struggle, Santa Cruz Cemetery is a historic site where more than 200 innocent civilians died when Indonesian troops turned violent during what was supposed to be a peaceful memorial procession. The historic event was filmed and photographed by two US journalists who themselves were beaten and bludgeoned during the massacre. The event set in motion the resistance against the Indonesian occupation. Address: Caicoli, Dili

Xanana Gusmao Reading Room

A library, museum and cultural center all rolled into one, the Xanana Gusmao Reading Room is an excellent place to discover the history of East Timor. The old colonial structure is an attraction itself and picture worthy.Address: Rua Belarmino Lobo City Centre Phone: +670-332-2831 Website: N/A

Tais Mercado
Tais is a piece of native cloth weaving which is indigent to East Timor that is produced in almost every region in the country. The Tais Market in the heart of Dili sells a variety of the products along with a wide range of pottery, old coins and other curios. Address: Rua Sebastiao da Costa, Caicoli

Dili Wharf
The main starting point of almost every excursion in East Timor, the Dili Wharf is another must-see attraction not only known for its stunning views of ship wrecks and breathtaking sunsets, but for its proximity to other sites in town, such as the Motael Church (which is the oldest in the country) and the Integration Monument. Colorful markets are also only a short walk away. Address: Dili Waterfront

Volunteering

Timor-Leste only regained its freedom in 2002 after a long and brutal occupation. As a newly independent country there is a lot for the

Government to do in terms of nation building and meeting the day to day needs of the Timorese people.

Many organisations, both larger and more grass roots, welcome the assistance of volunteers in a wide range of roles and sectors including healthcare, handicrafts, farming and education.

If you would like a more in depth experience of Timor-Leste and its people start making enquiries. Contact your country's respective embassy in Timor-Leste or search online.

Destination

Municipalities

Timor-Leste is a fascinating and extremely photogenic country to explore offering travelers a wide variety of experiences. Timor-Leste has thirteen municipalities (administrative regions) each with different landscapes, history and cultural traditions. Bobonaro, Liquicia, Dili, Manatuto, Baucau and Lautem are located on the north coast. Dili municipality includes the nation's capital city of Dili, approximately 240,000 people, and Atauro Island lying to the north across Wetar Strait. Over the mountain ranges from Dili on the south coast are found Cova-Lima, Ainaro, Manufahi and Viqueque municipalities. Aileu and Ermera both are landlocked and Oecusse-Ambeno is in the western part of Timor surrounded by Indonesian territory and the Savu Sea.

Atauro (Dili)

Located enticingly close to Dili, Atauro Island is well suited for a day trip, or longer stay. Atauro is a wonderfully friendly and relaxing destination. While it is the perfect place to laze in a hammock, there is also a lot to enjoy if you want to be more active.

With rugged mountains, forests and grassy slopes, the coastline varies from overhanging cliffs to the most sublime beaches. Most of the Island is surrounded by reefs rich in marine life with crystal clear waters.

Atauro has the greatest diversity of reef fish and coral species anywhere in the world and the snorkelling and diving is excellent. Whales and dolphins can be seen year round with the best viewing during the seasonal migration.

The hills and coastline offer great hiking from a guided climb of Mt Manukoko to coastal walks.

On Atauro there is some lovely eco-accommodation and a good range of locally produced handicrafts. These include carved wooden figurines, Boneka dolls and bags and intricately woven reed mats and baskets.

Liquica

Liquica municipality lying to the west of Dili has an attractive coastline interspersed with rocky headlands, coves and beaches. These offer good swimming and the coral reefs provide excellent diving opportunities.

There are small towns dotted along the coast road and roadside vendors selling local produce from the hills beyond. The majority of local people speak Tocodede.

Timor-Leste's colonial past is very evident in this municipality with the remnants of a large historic jail at Aipelo and many fine Portuguese buildings in Liquica, the main administrative centre.

Further to the west, past a salt lake known for its pelicans, is the interesting small town of Maubara. In addition to many old Portuguese buildings it has an impressive 17th century Dutch Fort which is a must see. Across the road local women in bright blue bungalows produce handicrafts including colourful intricately woven baskets and other items.

Continuing past Maubara the road clings to the rocky coast and climbs high above the sea. It is a good location to look out for whales and dolphins especially in the migrating season as they often come in very close to the shore here. The views out towards the large island of Alor across the Savu Sea also are spectacular

Covalima

Covalima municipality is located in Timor-Leste's south west corner and borders both Indonesia and the Timor Sea. It lies across the rugged mountain hinterland from Dili. With very steep hill country, wide river valleys and lush coastal flats, it has the sprawling town of Suai as its main centre. The extremely large Suai Cathederal is an impressive local landmark.

The Covalima coast is characterised by salty marshlands, important for wildlife, and spectacular black sand beaches offering expansive vistas out to the Timor Sea.

Most people living in Covalima speak Tetun Terik or Bunak.

Ermera

The winding road up from Dili to centrally located Ermera municipality is perfect for road touring and mountain biking it offers expansive views out to Atauro Island.

In general, Ermera municipality is very rugged country and sparsely populated. It is the coffee producing heart of Timor-Leste. With steep hills covered in coffee forest, looking towards towering Mt Ramelau in the south often all that can be seen of most towns is their colourful church spires poking out through the trees.

Coffee is a shade loving plant which flourishes beneath the large canopied albezia trees. During the harvest season local people can be seen picking the ripe red coffee cherries that are then spread along the sides of the road and anywhere else flat they can find for drying in the hot sunshine.

Down on the lush, green river flats tropical fruit and vegetables are grown around the main towns of Gleno and Ermera and local market days are colourful and interesting social occasions with people often coming considerable distances from the surrounding villages. Examples of Portuguese architecture can be seen in the old town of Ermera.

On the western flanks of Mt Ramelau, Letefoho is a pretty village with a combination of Portuguese architecture and traditional Timorese houses. An alternative approach to climbing Mt Ramelau can be arranged from here. Further to the south lie the small market town of

Atsabe and the nearby Bandeira waterfall, the highest in Timor-Leste and an impressive sight in the wet season.

Baucau

Baucau municipality lies in the eastern part of Timor-Leste and includes its second largest city also named Baucau. Set on a breezy plateau overlooking the sea, Baucau has a new town centre with bustling sprawling market and an older centre with a much more sedate air. The attractive older part of town derives a decidedly Portuguese flavour from the Pousada de Baucau and other colonial buildings, some restored such as the beautiful old market square. This area is backed by steep limestone outcrops and shaded by large banyan tree and rustling palms. A clear freshwater spring feeds the large municipal swimming pool a great place to enjoy a refreshing dip.

Down the winding road from Baucau, there is the small village of Osolata and an absolutely breathtakingly beautiful coastline of white sand coves and beaches, stretching both west and east.

From the Baucau plateau impressive mountain ranges including Mt Matebian (2315m) dominate the skyline. This 'Mountain of Spirits' is protected and considered sacred by the Timorese people. Climbing towering Mt Matebian with a guide from Baguia, or one of the other small villages on its flanks, is a strenuous undertaking. Towards the summit stunted alpine vegetation gives way to wind sculptured fluted rock pinnacles and hikers are rewarded with stunning views of the eastern part of Timor-Leste and also back towards Mt Ramelau across Mundo Perdido.

Driving through the rolling Baucau plateau some areas seem almost untouched while others are used for cattle grazing and growing crops such as rice and corn. Wonderful fresh fruit and vegetables are available from roadside stalls.

The Portuguese-era mountain retreat of Venilale lying further to the south has impressive colonial architecture and offers good views, especially of Mt Matebian to the east. Nearby there also are located both the Vaicana natural hot springs and old excavated tunnels, a remnant of Japan's occupation during WWII.

Bobonaro

Bobonaro municipality lies in the far west of Timor-Leste bordering Indonesia and the Savu Sea. Along its northern coastline, beautiful sweeping grey sand beaches can be enjoyed from the road linking Dili and the Batugade border crossing.

The scenery varies from red earth and dryish vegetation reminiscent of northern Australia to bright green rice fields with water buffalo on the river flats. Clusters of food stalls selling grilled meat and fish, dried salt and other produce are at times encountered.

At Batugade there is a small salt water lake and an overgrown Portuguese fort.

Further inland up in the forested hills is located the small village of Balibo. The site of several massacres during the Indonesian occupation included one in which the 'Balibo Five' (2 Australians, 2 British and 1 New Zealander) were executed while attempting to film the initial invasion. These events are commemorated at Balibo House (a community centre) and in the nearby Portuguese Fort which has been converted into a small hotel and museum.

Maliana, the capital of Bobonaro sits amidst a fertile flood plain and is an important area for rice growing and other horticulture. The town's buildings are Portuguese influenced and there is a sprawling market. It is home to the Kemak people, whose rectangular stilt houses dot the countryside.

This inland basin is surrounded by some very steep mountains with limestone outcrops and caves. High on the flanks of Mt Loilako and the other mountains, the cone shaped thatched houses of the Tetun people can be seen. In this area there are some excellent guided hiking and cave exploring opportunities.

Bobonaro municipality also is famed for producing some very fine tais, many with distinctive black backgrounds.

The rugged country further south is covered in forest and open grasslands used for grazing cattle and horses and requires a strong 4WD vehicle. There are some fantastic views out to the south coast near to the old and dilapidated colonial retreat of Bobonaro and geo-thermal hot springs are found downhill from the small village of Marobo. These natural springs have been developed into a series of bathing pools.

A very rough road continues on to Zumalai on the south coast. Driving conditions are slow but the expansive scenic views and traditional villages along the way definitely make it worthwhile.

Dili

Dili municipality includes the nation's capital city, beaches to the east and west and the island of Atauro lying across Wetar Strait to the north. The capital also known as Dili is undergoing a rapid transformation with the development of new buildings and services following past destruction.

Dili nestles at the base of surrounding hills which are lush and green in the rainy season, revealing terracotta coloured earth in the dry. The city faces the ocean and is linked by a beachfront road and the waterfront with government buildings, Motael Church, a lighthouse and embassies. There is a pedestrian walkway along the central harbour, statues and small municipal gardens in which to relax shaded by large banyan trees. Vendors sell local crafts, tropical fruits, fresh seafood and refreshing green coconut juice. In the weekends and late afternoon you can watch an informal game of football or beach volley ball.

Due to its compactness, Dili is relatively easy to get around on foot and by taxi. It is a great place to recharge in between adventures in the districts. It is a pleasant and laid-back city with a good range of accommodation, restaurants, bars, shopping and attractions. The Timorese Resistance Archive and Museum is definitely worth a visit.

Many of the main restaurants and bars are located along the beachfront road (Avenida de Portugal) and out towards Areia Branca (white sands). The most popular of the city's beaches, Areia Branca has a number of beachside eateries and bars perfect for watching the sun set behind the island of Alor. Further on from Areia Branca is the statue of Cristo Rei perched on Cape Fatucama Dili's most famous landmark. Excellent views towards the city and over to Back Beach reward those climbing to the top.

At the western entrance to Dili on a headland near the Tasi Tolu Lakes is another large bronze statue celebrating Pope Paul II.

Visiting Dare up in the hills is also recommended with its WWII memorial and views across the city and out to Atauro Island.

Lautem

The most eastern municipality of Timor-Leste, Lautem includes the sprawling main centre of Lospalos and has a wealth of natural and cultural locations of interest to travellers.

Lospalos is home to the Fataluku people and they speak Fataluku (a Papuan language). They also are known for producing high quality tais, wood carvings and woven basket ware.

Portuguese architectural influences and remnants of colonial fortifications can be seen. However most notable are the tall elongated traditional Fataluku spirit houses which are constructed with a high tapering thatched roof a top stilts. These traditional spirit houses, like many of the local graves, are often adorned with animist symbols.

If you happen upon a festival featuring traditional dance and music while visiting Lautem, as in many other parts of Timor-Leste, you are in for a real treat.

Set on an undulated plain surrounded by forested hills the countryside around Lospalos is used for rice cultivation and other crops. Raising livestock, especially extensive herds of cattle and water buffalo is a main activity. Further towards the mountains and the south coast the municipality becomes wilder and more scarcely populated.

The 1,230sq/km eastern end of Lautem has been designated as part of the Nino Konis Santana National Park. This includes rugged forested ranges, the large salt water Lake Ira Lalaro, coastal beaches and offshore reefs, plus exquisite Jaco Island.

The small fishing village of Com adjoins the park's western boundary and has beautiful deserted creamy white sand beaches. Com is a great place to go fishing or to relax and watch the sunset from your accommodation.

From Tutuala's high cliff setting, views are mind blowing over the forested ranges, out to the Indonesian island of Kisar, and to the blue sea shimmering far below. From the local pousada's ramparts, rich birdlife can be observed along with monkeys swinging through the forest.

The limestone caves and buttresses within the national park have some of Timor-Leste's most important archeological treasures ancient fossils and cave drawings. To access the caves, guides can be arranged. The park's landscape is wild, unspoilt and rugged offering great terrain for these cave visits and other guided hiking.

At the very tip of Lautem lies the small island gem of Jaco across a shallow channel from beautiful Valu beach. It is easy to reach with the local fishermen in their colourful craft. Jaco Island is sacred to the Timorese people and no development or overnight stays are allowed. As a result it is a totally natural setting where the whitest sand is lapped by the clearest and most azure ocean. In addition to sublime swimming, snorkelling and diving, the Jaco experience is also about enjoying the solitude of this special place

Aileu

Located in the central highlands immediately to the south of Dili, Aileu includes very steep forested ridges some lush with tropical vegetation and others dry and rocky, covered in sparse eucalyptus trees and grasses. Beautiful rice paddy ribbons run along the river valleys between the steep slopes making a colourful contrast with the mountain ranges behind.

On the winding road from Dili, travellers often stop to capture the expansive views down to the winding rivers far below and out to the northern coast with Atauro Island in the distance. Apart from the villages located close to the road and on ridge tops, others are hidden from view by the steep terrain and forest.

Going further south into the municipality the road from Dili eventually drops down to a very picturesque fertile high land valley and the bustling market town of Aileu. If it is market day, take a break and see all the fresh vegetable and fruit on display, plus coffee, tobacco and other local produce. There is a small freshwater lake to the town's west. Continuing on south towards Maubisse the countryside starts to feel even wilder and more remote. The views are magnificent and in the wet season enjoy the wild flowers along the roadside. Traditional thatched roof villages can be seen in the distance, either linked by road or walking track.

Ainaro

Ainaro municipality, in the southern part of the country, has spectacular scenery from the central mountains to the wild south coast and provides wonderful opportunities for exploring and hiking. This area includes Timor-Leste's highest peak Mt Ramelau (2960m) which is sacred to the Timorese and known at Tatamailau (grandfather). The towns of Maubisse and Hato Builico have very spectacular hill settings and the larger town of Ainaro is located at much lower elevation in a lush river valley midway to the Timor Sea.

This is definitely scenery where you want to keep your camera close at hand. The panoramic views from the Maubisse pousada on its promontory are especially impressive, as are the views from Mt Ramelau at dawn after a guided climb from Hato Builico. Looking out over the mountain ranges of Timor-Leste bathed in the early morning light is an unforgettable and very rewarding experience.

A lot of coffee is grown in the Ainaro area and vegetables are cultivated in between rocky screes on what often seems like impossibly steep slopes. Ponies are still commonly used for carrying produce and other goods between the isolated villages and markets. They and other livestock are seen grazing on the mountain sides.

The majority of the local people speak Mambae and their villages with characteristic thatched circular, conical roofed houses are scattered across the municipality.

Manufahi

Manufahi municipality stretches from the central mountains to the southern coast. Inland, scenic vistas of the large mountains and expansive valleys are magnificent. Small villages can be found along the roads and on isolated ridges.

Travelling south, the road from Dili winds down steeply after Aituto and follows a lush green river valley towards Same, the administrative capital of Manufahi. The local climate and terrain are well suited to the cultivation of many tropical fruits and vegetables, plus Timor-Leste's famous organically grown coffee.

Same offers a great base for exploring the surrounding areas. A trek to Mt Kablaki through dense forests and small villages is an ideal way to experience the natural beauty of the area and the nearby river is good for swimming. Same also has some lovely old Portuguese buildings.

From Same the road continues on further south to Betano, a small fishing village on the coast with long sweeping black sand beaches. This was the location where Australian Sparrow Force guerrilla troops had to be evacuated by ship and submarine during WWII.

Much of the coastal area known as Sungai Clere further to the east of Betano have been proposed for protection as a wildlife sanctuary. This wetland area and the hill country inland area to its north are very isolated and often inaccessible by road in the wet season.

The majority of people living in Manufahi speak Mambae and their traditional circular thatched buildings can be seen.

Oecusse-Ambeno

Located in the western part of Timor, Oecusse-Ambeno municipality is separated from the rest of Timor-Leste by Indonesian territory which surrounds the enclave except to the north where it borders the Savu Sea. Oecusse-Ambeno recently has been designated a Special Social Market Economic Zone (ZEESM) by the Timor-Leste Government and large scale infrastructure development and building construction is underway.

Lifau near the main coastal town of Pante Macassar was the first place the Portuguese landed in 1515 and this site is marked by a memorial park. The most interesting other colonial site and a good viewing point is an old garrison building Fatusuba on a hilltop immediately behind the town.

In 1959 when Portugal and the Netherlands divided Timor Island under the Treaty of Lisbon, Oecusse-Ambeno remained with the Portuguese section, now known as Timor-Leste.

The laid back town of Pante Macassar is fronted by a grey sand beach and is overlooked by striking mountain peaks. The groves of banana, coconut, papaya and mango trees between the houses give it a very tropical air.

Pantai Mahata just to the east of Pante Macassar has a good reef for snorkelling and diving as well as offering an excellent vantage point for the annual whale migration.

This isolated enclave features jagged mountain ranges, fertile river flats along the Tono River and long sweeping beaches great for beach walking, swimming and surf casting.

This municipality offers some wonderful hiking opportunities including the area around Kutet with its dense jungle, waterfalls and mountain panoramas. Walking tracks link the many traditional villages and a hiking guide is definitely required.

To the south of Oecusse-Ambeno, the enclave is ringed by a mountainous escarpment with peaks rising to more than 1,200m. In this area near Oesilo geothermal small hot mud volcanoes can be found blowing their tops.

The local population of Oecusse-Ambeno are mostly Dawan and are known for their incredible warmth and friendliness. Their traditional conical shaped houses dot the landscape from the coast to the mountains and they mostly speak Baikeno. They are acclaimed for producing distinctively woven and embroidered tais, as well as wood carvings and other crafts.

Manatuto

Manatuto municipality is located to the east of Dili and stretches across the entire country from a beautiful north coast of idyllic white sandy beaches, steep cliffs and mangroves bordering the Wetar Strait, to the wilder Timor Sea in the south. It is one of the country's least populated and most rugged municipalities with large braided rivers and a very mountainous hinterland. Much of the landscape and its villages have remained virtually unchanged for centuries. The majority of local people speak Galoli.

This area is known as the birthplace of Xanana Gusmao, the resistance leader elected as the nation's president in 2001 and who later became Timor-Leste's prime minister.

The large regional town of Manatuto, lying beside the Laclo River on the north coast, is regarded for its bustling Sunday market and also for terracotta pottery produced in local kilns. Further to the east, the small town of Laleia has a pretty pastel pink twin towered church, considered one of the most beautiful In Timor-Leste.

Along the north coast closer to Dili are well-known sites for diving and snorkelling and Dollar Beach is a popular swimming and picnicking location. Grilled fish and rice can be purchased from roadside stalls and at Manleo there is a good range of woven basketwork for sale.

Local farmers cultivate rice and other crops and graze livestock such as sheep and goats. Inland at higher elevation near Laclubar tree crops such as coffee and avocado are also grown.

The forests and coastal swamps near the isolated south coast have been proposed for designation as part of a wilder wildlife sanctuary that stretches west into neighbouring Manufahi municipality. Flooded each wet season this area known as Sungai Clere is rich with birdlife, including rare cockatoos and pigeons.

Viqueque

Viqueque municipality lies on the higher rainfall south coast of Timor-Leste and with its steep terrain, dense forest and rushing rivers offers a beautiful natural setting in which to explore.

The main road into Viqueque from Baucau itself is very scenic, crossing a high point with nearby rugged rock formations and providing great views of Mt Matebian to the east and Mundo Perdido to the west.

Mundo Perdido (1,775m), the 'Lost World' has Timor-Leste's largest tract of rainforest and is a protected area due to its rich plant, bird and animal life. Mundo Perdido also is a wonderful place for guided hiking. Fantastic views of the surrounding countryside can be seen from the ridges and it is interesting finding out how local people utilise the forest for food and materials. Such guided hiking and other activities including visiting nearby limestone caves and cooking lessons in a local village can all be easily organised when staying in accommodation at Loi Hunu located further to the south. The Loi Hunu River has rapids excellent for swimming and lovely big boulders to laze on.

If you are interested in learning more about the local Timorese resistance history there also are opportunities in this regard.

Viqueque the administrative centre is a largish regional town with guest houses and 'warungs' and has a nearby hot water spring. There is plenty of evidence of the Portuguese era architecture in Viqueque's schools and churches. Its surrounding farmland is used for growing rice, peanuts and other crops, plus livestock grazing.

The majority of local people speak either Macasae or Tetun Terik. They are well-known for their distinctive woven tais, coloured with dyes from local plants and berries.

Plan your Trip

Arriving in Timor-Leste

By Air

Getting to Timor-Leste by air is easy, with international flights from Denpasar (Bali), Darwin (Australia) and Singapore. Dili is just over an hour away from Darwin by plane.

On arrival at Presidente Nicolau Lobato International Airport, a Timor-Leste Tourist and Business Visas (USD30 for 30 days) is granted to holders of valid passports. (Note: Portuguese are visa exempt when travelling for tourism). When departing a USD10 airport departure tax is required.

Dili is a 10 minute drive from the airport. To get into the city prearrange a transfer with your accommodation, book the 24-hour Flybus airport shuttle (USD10 per person; Tel +670 7750 8585) or organise a taxi (around USD10). (Note: With yellow taxis do negotiate fares prior to commencing your trip).

By Land

Journeying over land between West Timor and Timor-Leste, there are daily air conditioned minibus services linking the capitals of Kupang and Dili via the border crossing near Batugade. It is an arduous 12 hour trip through beautiful rolling hill country and along the scenic coastline west of Dili. All nationalities, with exception of Portuguese and Indonesians, must obtain a Visa Application Authorization before arriving at the land border post. Apply in person at a Timor-Leste Embassy or Consulate (there is one in Denpasar +62 3 6123 5093 and Kupang, Tel +62 813 3936 7558) or online at the Ministry of Immigration website (allowing around 10 working days to receive a printable authorization). Then present this document and the USD30 fee to Immigration at the border crossing.

By Sea

While currently there are no regular scheduled passenger shipping services between neighbouring countries and Timor-Leste, recreational craft often stop in Dili and a few large passenger cruise ships are starting to ply Timorese waters. For those arriving by sea, Tourism and Business Visas (USD30 for 30 days stay) can be gained on arrival at the Sea Port in central Dili with presentation of valid passports. (Note: Portuguese travelling on Portuguese passports are visa exempt when travelling for tourism.)

Getting Around

By Rental Vehicle

Timor-Leste is an exciting country to explore and there is a lot to see out in the districts. Hiring a vehicle and driver is a great idea if you wish to travel flexibly and in comfort. With an experienced driver you are also more likely to stay on route (many road signs are lacking) and you'll learn much more.

Part of the adventure is definitely the roads, some of which are notorious with their blind corners and pot-holes. In general the north coast road is in good condition following a major upgrade from the Batugade border to Lospalos in the east, but the roads inland crossing the mountains to the south coast are variable.

Road access to Hato Builico (Mt Ramelau) and Valu (Jaco Island) requires a strong 4WD. While a standard car is fine for Dili and outskirts, hiring a 4WD is still definitely needed for travel further afield.

All companies can organise drivers and this is definitely recommended.

Motorcycles can also be hired by licensed riders. 4WD vehicles cost around $85-120 per day to rent and motorcycles cost $25-35.

If your preference is for other aspects of your trip to be organised also, such as accommodation, specialist Dili based tour operators are happy to arrange personalised itineraries refer to refer to the following website online http://www.timorleste.tl/what-to-do/exploring

By Bus (and other public transport)

Ornate, vividly painted buses (usually crowded) provide transport daily on the main routes from Dili to Maliana, Suai, and via Baucau to Viqueque and Lospalos. Schedules and trip times vary depending on the number of stops and road conditions.

Most public transport services leave early in the morning once they have filled up with passengers. Dili's bus departure points are on the city outskirts Becora for eastern districts, Taibessi central and southern and Tasi Tolu western.

Rugged routes to more isolated locations from these centres are covered by smaller microlets (mini-buses), bemos (vans) and anggunas (trucks carrying passengers and other belongings on the back) and in some cases ojeks motorcycle taxis which take pillion passengers.

On Atauro Island getting around usually involves hiring a tuktuk (auto rickshaw) for travel between Beloi and Vila-Maumeta, a 4WD vehicle for accessing Anartutu up in the mountains, or a boat for journeying around the coast.

The small colourful microlets operate on specified set routes around Dili, Baucau and other main towns. In Dili the microlets are numbered and each travels a set route. To get on hail from the roadside and to disembark tap your coin on the metal handrail and the driver will stop.

By Taxi

Taxis are a frequent sight on Dili's roads there are lots of them, but operation is primarily limited to daylight hours. City fares vary between $2-5 depending on the distance. Flag them down from the roadside or ask your accommodation to organise. Those that are available in the evenings charge higher rates and have to be contacted by phone.

With the yellow taxis, fares need to be negotiated prior to travel. In contrast the blue taxis provide a more consistent quality service, use taxi meters and are available in the evenings and early mornings if rung.

An airport minibus shuttle service is another option if travelling between the airport and Dili (must be pre-booked).

By Boat

Both Oecusse and Atauro are linked by regular passenger boat services from Dili.

Oecusse is serviced by the Government run, Nakroma ferry which departs Dili Sea Port twice a week (Monday and Thursday) and returns from Pante Macassar the day following. The ferry is usually crowded and the trip takes around 8-12 hours. For ferry tickets visit their office at the Dili Port. Dragon Star Shipping also runs daily services on their fast star craft between Dili and Pante Macassar, approximately 3-4 hours.

There are a number of passenger boats plying the Wetar Strait between Dili and Atauro Island. Services vary from daily water taxi services (approximately 90 mins travel) to the Nakroma ferry which operates Saturday only and takes around 3 hours. All services are weather dependent, bookings are essential and charters can be arranged.

From Dili, with the exception of the ferry and dragon star boat which depart the Sea Port, other services leave from the Dili waterfront, just to the east of Palacio do Governo. Returning from Atauro, departures are from Beloi.

On Atauro Island, boats can be organised between Beloi and other coastal villages, including Adara on the more isolated north coast. When boating keep a look out for whales and dolphins, as sightings are common. Seabirds and flying fish are other highlights.

At the eastern end of Timor-Leste, Jaco Island is only a short distance from the mainland and on arrival at Valu it is easy to arrange transportation with local fishermen.

Contact boat operators and Pante Macassar, Atauro and Valu accommodation directly for more information.

By Aircraft

Timor-Leste is a compact, mountainous country and flying greatly reduces travel time to Atauro, Oecusse, Suai, Maliana, Baucau, Lospalos and Same.

ZEESM, a Government Authority, operates a small aircraft between Dili and Pante Macassar, Oecusse on a scheduled daily basis (Thursday excluded). ZEESM can also arrange flight charters on this route and to other municipalities.

MAF (Mission Aviation Fellowship NGO) operates from the Dili International Airport using small aircraft (up to 7 passengers). While they primarily run a medical evacuation service for Timorese living in the districts, their planes can be chartered for tourism flights to Atauro and other destinations.

Accommodation

Accommodation in Timor-Leste comes in all styles and price ranges from the very comfortable to back to nature camping.

You'll find accommodation from modern international hotels and apartments to budget motels and backpackers in the laid back capital of Dili, with its very picturesque coastal location.

In the outlying districts options vary from small hotels in the bigger towns to guesthouses including historic pousadas, eco-lodges, homestays, camping and even religious compounds. Generally in the districts properties are smaller scale, offering comfortable but simple facilities, often in idyllic surroundings.

Many accommodation properties have their own restaurants and they can also advise on others nearby. When travelling independently in the more remote areas, it is advisable, when booking your accommodation, to also discuss meal arrangements.

Adara Eco-Resort (Mario's Place)
Simple thatched accommodation with shared bathroom, located besides a beautiful white sand beach on the remote west coast. All meals are included. Access is by boat or walking from Beloi. Guided walks, boat trips and snorkel gear hire. Relaxing place with fantastic sunsets.
Tel (+670) 7795 7272 / 7764 1196

Adara Eco-Safari Camp
Specialist dive camp next to Adara beach tents in thatched gazebos with shared bathrooms. Boat from Dili and all meals included. This is a great place for diving, snorkelling, yoga and beach walks. Excellent sunsets.
Tel (+670) 7723 0965/7723 0964

Arbiru Beach Resort
Accommodation has beachside location. Air conditioned apartments feature kitchenettes, open plan living, bedrooms (1-2) and bathrooms. Restaurant, bar, swimming pool and tour desk. Breakfast included. Free wifi and airport transfers.
Tel (+670) 332 2936 / 7726 3642

Atauro Dive Resort
Small personalised eco-resort beside Beloi beach with thatched bungalows and shared bathroom. Specialised scuba diving centre onsite. Breakfast included and other meals by arrangement. Great sunrises and very peaceful. Activities include diving, snorkelling, swimming and of course lying in a hammock.
Tel (+670) 7738 6166 / 7323 2455

Balibo Fort Hotel
Boutique hotel with restaurant and small museum built within a colonial era fort. Sweeping views across forested hills, Balibo village

and out to sea. Air conditioned bedrooms have ensuite bathrooms. Local walking guides and cave visits can be arranged. Free wifi. Breakfast included and other meals by arrangement.

Tel (+670) 7709 1555

Barry's Place
Eco-resort with spacious open air restaurant, thatched bungalows and shared bathrooms in tropical gardens beside the beach. Very relaxing. All meals included. Organizes activities/tours and rents snorkel gear/bikes/kayaks/fishing rods etc.

Tel (+670) 7723 6084 / 7744 1101

Beach Garden Hotel
Hotel has swimming pool and fitness centre. Air-conditioned bedrooms have private bathrooms. Apartments also available. Onsite restaurant, tour desk and self-service laundry. Free wifi, parking and buffet breakfast. Free airport shuttle service (longer stays only).

Tel (+670) 331 5888 / 332 5999 / 7743 6999 / 7333 8508

Beachside Hotel
Hotel with sea breeze and ocean views beside the beach. Bedrooms have ensuite bathrooms and some have kitchenettes. Breakfast included and wifi. Onsite café and gift shop. Swimming and beach walks. Sensational sunsets. Free parking.

Tel (+670) 7754 9681 / 7750 2184

Beloi Beach Hotel
Small hotel overlooking the ocean with restaurant/bar and swimming pool. Rooms have air conditioning and private bathrooms. All meals and motor-launch transport from Dili included. Organizes activities/tours and rents snorkel gear/bikes/fishing rods etc.
Tel (+670) 7558 3421

Beloi Beach House
Luxury camping next to Beloi beach. Boat from Dili and all meals included. Diving and other activities can be arranged.
Tel (+670) 7723 0965/7723 0964

Café Maubisse Guesthouse
Guesthouse set in garden has small lounges and balconies. Bedrooms have private bathrooms. Breakfast included and other meals by arrangement.
Tel (+670) 7727 4756

Caimeo Beach Resort
Beachside resort includes spacious bungalows and luxury camping with private bathrooms and Black Rock Restaurant. Good beach for swimming, expansive ocean views and fantastic place to enjoy the sunset. One hour's drive from Dili. Resort can help organise transport and airport pick-ups.
Tel (+670) 7798 8305

Casa Minha Backpackers

Backpacker accommodation shared dormitory rooms with single and bunk beds. Breakfast included and free wifi (public areas). Small restaurant onsite.

Tel (+670) 7719 8198

Caz Bar Seaside Villa

One bedroom air conditioned bungalow with private bathroom right next to the beach. Balcony has sea views. Onsite restaurant and bar. Breakfast included.

Tel (+670) 7723 3961

Costa Guesthouse

Guesthouse with beautiful ocean views and large veranda. Air-conditioned bedrooms have private bathrooms. Breakfast included.

Tel (+670) 7724 8423 / 7764 4508

D'City Hotel

Air conditioned bedrooms with private bathrooms. On-site restaurant and small fitness centre. Free wifi and airport shuttle service.

Tel (+670) 332 2653 / 7339 3922

Dili Central Backpackers

Air conditioned dormitory rooms and share bathrooms. Lounge, kitchen and tour desk. Free breakfast and wifi. Onsite bar and gift shop. Bike and motorbike hire available.

Tel (+670) 7350 6279

Dili Homestay/Guesthouse

Comfortable Portuguese style homestay in quiet private setting. Meals and drinks available on request.

Tel (+670) 7774 7524

Discovery Inn

Charming small air-conditioned hotel with restaurant and bar. Breakfast included. Bedrooms have ensuite bathrooms. Onsite gift shop. Free airport shuttle service and wifi.

Tel (+670) 331 1111

DTL Guesthouse

DTL Guest House has choice of air conditioned studio apartments and guest houses available with lounge/kitchen, bedroom(s) and private bathroom. Swimming pool and free wifi. Dive centre and Castaways restaurant/bar on site.

Tel (+670) 7723 7092

Excelsior Resort

Air conditioned suites and bedrooms with ensuite bathrooms. Restaurant and swimming pool. Free buffet breakfast and wifi. Conference facilities also available. Free airport shuttle (longer stays only).

Tel (+670) 332 1118 / 7760 8333

Green Diamond Residence
Air conditioned apartments with bedrooms, kitchen and bathroom. Swimming pool and fitness centre. Free wifi, parking and airport shuttle service. Bike hire is available.

Tel (+670) 7736 2449

Hakmatek Eco-accommodation
Eco-accommodation located in countryside near Maubisse. Beautiful views and peaceful setting. Bedrooms with thatched roofs and share bathrooms. Breakfast included and other meals by arrangement. Hiking guides and village visits can be organised.

Tel (+670) 7751 3490

Hato Builico Homestay
Homestay with bedrooms/share bathroom. Meals can be organised. Host (English speaking) is available as trekking guide.

Tel (+670) 7736 8515 / 7618 5904

Hotel Comunitaria Wailakurini
Guesthouse in the countryside on the banks of the Loi Hunu River. Breakfast included and other meals by arrangement. Rooms have ensuite bathrooms. Activities nearby include guided trekking on Mundo Perdido, caves exploring, cooking lessons in local village and

learning about resistance history.

Tel (+670) 7656 0577/7783 2287/7757 6871

Hotel Esplanada
Beachfront location, restaurant, bar and swimming pool. Air-conditioned bedrooms with ensuite bathrooms. Free parking and wifi.

Tel (+670) 3313 088 / 7772 5272

Hotel Lecidere
Air conditioned rooms with private bathrooms. Onsite restaurant. Breakfast included, free parking and wifi.

Tel (+670) 332 5083 / 7364 3955

Hotel Roberto Carlos
Accommodation has restaurant and bar onsite. Bedrooms have private bathrooms. Breakfast included.

Tel (+670) 7724 0627 / 7723 0826

Lakumorre Guesthouse
Guesthouse is set amidst shady trees besides a beautiful beach. Choice of bedrooms with private bathrooms or share bedrooms/bathrooms. Camping sites available. Breakfast and other meals by arrangement. Boat transport to Jaco Island, hiking guides and caves visits can be organised.

Tel (+670) 7724 5620

Manukoko Rek
Accommodation ranges from thatched huts with shared bathroom, to larger rooms with private bathrooms. Restaurant specializes in Italian food with pizza and freshly made pasta. Breakfast is included. There is a good beach nearby, just a few minutes' walk away.
Tel (+670) 7748 7301 / 7795 5692

Moby's Hotel
Waterfront accommodation includes private rooms and backpacker share dormitory accommodation. Free parking and onsite restaurant and gift shop. Bike hire available. Breakfast included (some rooms).
Tel (+670) 7833 9050

Novo Turismo Resort & Spa
Modern air conditioned hotel on waterfront with swimming pool, spa pool, fitness centre and spa/wellness centre. Bedrooms/suites have private bathrooms. Restaurant, café/bar and conference facilities. Free wifi and airport shuttle.
Tel (+670) 331 0005

Oecusse Amasat
Guesthouse with restaurant/bar located opposite beach. Air conditioned bedrooms have private bathrooms. Breakfast included and other meals by arrangement. Hiking guides and snorkelling can be

organised.

Tel (+670) 7732 9755

Safety & Health

Crocodiles

With the exception of Atauro, Timor-Leste does have estuarine crocodiles around its coast and on the rare cases attacks happen, they are often fatal. Prior to going near the water, it is a sensible precaution to check with the locals whether the area is safe for swimming and if crocodiles have been recently sighted.

Driving

It is recommended when hiring a vehicle that you employ a driver unless you are experienced with local Timor-Leste driving conditions. Do buckle up seat belts and if travelling by motorcycle or bicycle wear a helmet. Also please keep your speed down, especially when travelling through villages as children often play near the road. To hire vehicles (including motorcycles) driving licences are required.

Food and Water

Take normal travel precautions when eating food and drinking Timor-Leste tap water is not safe to drink unless boiled or chemically treated. Bottled water is readily available.

Health Precautions

Before visiting Timor-Leste consult your doctor, or travel clinic, regarding vaccinations needed and do bring a good medical kit, as health services are limited, especially in the districts. It is important to take out comprehensive health insurance that covers all your intended activities (e.g. diving, mountain biking) and provides for evacuation if needed.

Health services:

Dili National Hospital +670 331 0541

Stamford Clinic +670 311 0141 / 331 1209

Bairo Pite Clinic +670 7723 8343

Climate

Timor-Leste is a hot and humid country, around 25-35C and the sunshine can be very intense. If arriving from somewhere cooler, it is important to avoid dehydration by drinking plenty of water, replacing salt lost from perspiration and limiting activity in the middle of the day as you adapt to the increased temperature. Covering up is also recommended to prevent sunburn.

Mosquitoes

In Timor-Leste there is a risk of mosquito borne diseases including dengue and to a much lesser extent malaria, especially in the wet season. It is recommended you apply insect repellent and cover up at all times of the day and evening.

Ocean Currents

Some popular sites for diving, snorkelling and swimming can experience very strong currents and care needs to be taken when in the water as conditions can change quickly.

Security

Before visiting Timor-Leste do check out the recent travel advisory posted by your relevant country. In general Timor-Leste is rated similar to many other South-East Asian countries. That said, do avoid situations where there are crowds gathering or protests and please don't flash money or leave valuables lying around. In Dili, if heading out after dark, do have a plan to get back to your accommodation as there is poor street lighting and no taxis (unless prearranged). For security reasons it is advised in Timor-Leste you travel with a companion (or guide) and don't visit isolated areas or travel at night.

Visa & Immigration

Everyone likes a smooth travel experience. Also it is frequently the small parts that matter! Particularly when things work the same way from one nation to another, like cash matters, transport frameworks, visa standards and regulations, as well as the weather. This is the reason we've assembled here everything you have to think about when travelling to East Timor. Below you will find fundamental information that will help you to get around without breaking a sweat.

Visa Requirements

East Timor allows all citizens of states that are contracting parties to the Schengen Agreement to stay without a visa for a maximum period of 90 days in any 180-day period.

There is also a visa exemption for holders of diplomatic or service passports of China.

If visitors arrive at a land border (except for Indonesian and Portuguese nationals), they must apply in advance for a Visa Application Authorization which is then presented to an immigration official at the border. If other conditions are met a single or multiple entry visa valid for up to 90 days is granted for a fee of US$30. Travellers applying in advance may be granted a visa valid for up to 90 days stay, which can be valid for single or multiple entries.

Look at the Immigration Department of East Timor, and particularly the connection to the Tourist Visa for items on visa prerequisites, and for portions on the best way to request a "visa requisition authorization" (which may be got via email before you travel), or how to seek a visa at an Embassy or Consulate if you need to enter from a land/sea border crossing. Apart from Tourist & Business Visas, different visas are accessible and include Transit Visa, Working Visa, Studying Visa, Cultural, Scientific, Sport & Media Visa and Residence Visa. To be granted a Traveller Visa the following requirements should be met, as expressed by the Immigration Department of East Timor.

The traveller should:

- ✓ Show plan of stay or a genuine visit interest (as vacationer or business excursion).

- ✓ Show sufficient funds for time of proposed stay (access to Us$100 on passage & Us$50 for every day).

- ✓ Exhibit arranged accommodation, hold a return ticket or indicate the capacity to reserve one on its own.

Visitors are likely to be surveyed as being of great character and health before they will be allowed the visa or allowed to enter East Timor. All outsiders trying to enter East Timor on a brief visa are asked to have a valid national identification (passport) with an expiry date at least 6 months from the date of entrance into East Timor and should have no less than one clear page accessible for Visa stamp.

When you seek a Visa on landing, the visa will be conceded for the term of stay up to 30 days, and is good for a single entry. If you wish to extended the stay, the cost is US$35 for up to 30 days, or US$75 for between 30 and 60 days. Extension of a tourist visa past 30 days requires a patron (also known as a sponsor), an East Timorese national or work-permit holder, who should complete a "Termo de Responsabilidade" (which stands for "Term of Responsibility", basically stating that the person will be responsible for you, ensuring your behavior and consistence with East Timorese laws for the length of time of your stay).

The individuals who apply ahead of time for a visitor visa at an Embassy or Consulate, or who apply via email coordinated with the Immigration Department for a "visa application authorization" might request a visa permit up to 90 days, with single or numerous entrances. Guests are encouraged to hold the essential amount of money in US Dollars for the cost of the visa expenses upon landing at the airport/arriving at the border. The ATMs available at the airport are placed after the immigration office, so guests must have US$30 in cash to pay for their visa. Portuguese passport holders don't require a visa for short stays (max 90 days).

Loss of passport

If you lose your international identification (passport, national identity card) while in East Timor, please make a police report promptly and approach your government office in Dili to seek a replacement document.

Popular Locations

Timor-Leste is an intriguing new tourism destination and attracting an increasing number of international travellers keen to experience its coral reefs, beaches, rugged mountains and rich cultural heritage.

Those already holidaying in Timor-Leste are drawn for many reasons from desire for a relaxing short break somewhere different to wanting to go exploring in a new destination off the beaten track by 4WD and motorbike. Many have a specific interest they wish to pursue culture and history, diving, hiking, whale and dolphin watching, mountain biking and birding.

All municipalities of Timor-Leste have something special to offer travellers and to help you plan your trip we've identified Timor-Leste's most popular locations

Atauro
Why Visit

Atauro Island offers world class diving and snorkelling on its fantastic reefs. Recent research shows Atauro Island has the highest diversity of reef fish and coral species of anywhere on earth.

It is also perfect for beach relaxing, swimming and hiking. It has a very friendly, hospitable and welcoming vibe.

Boat access from Dili can be easily arranged and there is a good range of accommodation including small eco-resorts available

Municipality: Atauro (Dili)

Balibo
Why Visit

The small hill-town of Balibo near the land border in the western part of Timor-Leste has an old fort which provides expansive views of the surrounding country side. Within the fort is a boutique hotel and restaurant. At the hotel guided visits to local villages and caves can be organised. Across the road from the fort, Balibo House provides information on what happened during the Indonesian occupation, including the massacre of the Balibo Five

Municipality: Bobonaro

Baucau
Why Visit

Baucau lying to the east of Dili has an old town with a charmingly raffish air due to its colonial buildings and huge banyan trees. There is a beautiful old swimming pool fed from a clear natural spring and the flamboyant pink Pousada de Baucau overlooks the town centre.

Baucau is Timor-Leste's second biggest centre and has a range of accommodation and restaurants available. Down at the sea a short drive from Baucau you'll find a small fishing village and a spectacular coastline of white sand beaches and rocky coves

Municipality: Baucau

COM
Why Visit

Com is a small fishing village on the western edge of the Nino Konis Santana National Park in Lautem. It has beautiful creamy white beaches stretching in both directions. A small resort and guest houses line the beachfront. Activities such as fishing can be arranged. It has a relaxing, serene air and is the perfect place to enjoy Timor-Leste's magnificent tropical sunsets

Municipality: Lautem

Jaco, Valu & Tutuala
Why Visit

Jaco Island lies across from Valu, a lovely beach area backed by forested limestone escarpments, at the far eastern tip of Timor-Leste. Sacred Jaco Island is a tropical paradise. Its transparent waters teem with underwater life and offer fantastic diving, snorkelling and swimming.

Day access to the Island is by small fishing boat. Accommodation at Valu ranges from eco-camping to guest houses. Guided trips through the forest to the local caves within the Nino Konis Santana National Park are another highlight.

The drive down to Valusere from Tutuala is very steep in places and requires a 4WD vehicle. At the top of the Tutuala escarpment from the local pousada the views out to sea and across the forested ranges of the national park are stunning
Municipality: Lautem.

Maubara & Liquica
Why Visit

Maubara and Liquica are two coastal towns located an easy drive west of Dili. Timor-Leste's colonial past is very apparent with many Portuguese buildings and a Dutch fort. Maubara is known for its skilled basket weavers. There are small resorts and other accommodation

along this coast and the beaches offer good swimming and diving
Municipality: Liquica

Mt Ramelau & Hato Builico
Why Visit

A highlight for many of a holiday in Timor-Leste is a guided hike from the village of Hato Builico, located high in the Tatamailau range (2000m), to the summit of Mt Ramelau to watch the sun rise.

In all directions the views are stunning. Other guided hikes also can be organised in the surrounding valleys and to nearby traditional villages from the guest houses. A good 4WD vehicle or motorbikes are needed to access Hato Builico due to the steep mountainous terrain.
Municipality: Ainaro

Maubisse
Why Visit

Maubisse is perched on a ridge at a height of around 1400m in rugged mountains and is surrounded by spectacular scenery. It's an old hill town and makes a delightful break from the heat and humidity of the coast.

Guided walks can be arranged to traditional Mambae villages and it is a good place to learn more about coffee growing. Guest houses available include the fine old Maubisse pousada offering expansive views.

Municipality: Ainaro

Marobo
Why Visit

The Marobo geothermal hot springs are located near Bobonaro in beautiful mountain country. Lying back in the hot water pools having a soak looking out over the valley is a very blissful experience.

Most visitors travel up from their accommodation in Maliana or Balibo by motorbike or 4WD vehicle.

Municipality: Bobonaro

Loi Hunu, Mundo Perdido & Mt Matebian
Why Visit

Inland from Baucau, Loi Hunu lies in lush countryside. The drive there is quite beautiful with impressive views of Mt Matebian and other ranges along the way. At Loi Hunu it is very relaxing and there is refreshing swimming in the nearby river.

It is also a great location for organising a guided hike of Mundo Perdido, a mountain range with dense rainforest and rich bird life.

The guesthouse owners are also happy to arrange hikes to limestone caves and other locations of importance during the Timorese resistance, plus cooking lessons in the nearby village. Climbing Mt Matebian (2315m) can be organised from Baguia and other villages on its flanks.

Municipality: Baucau, Viqueque

Same
Why Visit

Same is located in a lush tropical river valley, part way between Timor-Leste's highest mountains and the wild south coast (Tasi Mane). Same is an excellent location for hiking Mt Kablaki, swimming in the nearby river and general relaxation.

The town has some interesting old Portuguese buildings and is an easy drive to Betano on the coast with its sweeping black sand beaches. Same has some good accommodation.

Municipality: Manufahi

Food and Restaurants

Splurging on good food will hardly put a dent in your budget in East Timor. Restaurant menus are most likely to offer traditional Asian curries and mouthwatering dishes made with fragrant spice pastes and crisp fried fare. Fresh grilled seafood is a staple in seaside villages, while local joints specialize in dishes with Papuan influences. Rice is an important part of the Timorese diet and is a side to most items. Local specialties like *ikan sabuko*, Spanish mackerel marinated in tamarind, basil and capsicum served with *budu* (tomato, mint, Spanish onion and lime sauce) and *batar daan* (a side dish made with corn, pumpkin and mung beans) are regular staples. *Tapai*, a fermented rice dish, is a local delicacy with a sweet, sour and faintly alcoholic taste. Coffee is the chief cash crop of East Timor, so organic blends are widely available in both restaurants and pubs.

Bars and Pubbing in East Timor

Nightlife in the capital is centered around beachfront bars that stay open late. Many local food joints and restaurants including inner-city places like *Diya* (Discovery Inn, Avenida Presidente Nicolau Lobato, Dili), *Gion* (Rua Belarmino Lobo 2-E, Ailelehun, Dili) and *Nautilaus* (Beach Road, Dili) serve until late, but nightlife is livelier along the coast. *Caz Bar* (Area Branca, Dili) is frequented by those who love late night barbeque, hamburgers and sizzling garlic prawns paired with an ice cold beer.

Castaway Bar (Avenida de Portugal/Motadel, Dili) is popular with expats in town. It specializes in a long beer and cocktail list, and is best known for its giant margarita. A shelf of books (mostly in English) is be found on site which you are encouraged to take or leave, backpacker style. Other expat bars include *One More Bar* (Rua Governador Filomena da Camara/Lecidere, Dili) and *Roo Bar* (Rua Pres. Nicolau Lobato, Dili). while the Meti Aut area is home to the famous *Atlantic Bar and Grill*, one of the newest establishments in the city.

Dining and Cuisine in East Timor

There is more than a handful of great restaurants to visit in Dili, many of which are found near the coast that offer not only exquisite food, but stunning views of the vast blue waters. *Terrace Cafe* (Rua Formosa, Central Dili) is a popular stopover for workers and students, where you can enjoy Padang-style meals on a breezy, ambient terrace. Also in the heart of Dili is *Rock Garden* (Central Dili), known for its mixture of Japanese, Filipino and Asian cuisine. *Gion* (Rua Belarmino Lobo 2-E, Ailelehun, Dili) is the place to go to for authentic Japanese dishes, while *Denpasar Moon* lets you indulge in a variety of Indonesian dishes.

Seaside restaurants like *Atasquinha* are popular for grilled fish dishes, along with *Seahorse Restaurant*, which is known for Balinese style cooking. *Kebab Club* (Rua Belarmino Lobo/Lecidere, Dili) is the place to go to for Turkish cravings in East Timor. There are many other notable restaurants in town, such as *Golden Star*(Avenida Liberdade de Imprensa, Dili), *Restaurante Sagres*, *Vasco da Gama*, and *Bagan Beach Cafe Restaurant*(Avenida de Portugal/Kampung Alor, Beach Road, Dili).

Shopping and Leisure
Shopping & Services

Dili's shopping options range from Timor Plaza (modern shopping mall) to smaller businesses, markets and roadside kiosks. There is a wide selection of goods available including handicrafts refer Arts & Crafts. When travelling to the municipalities do take what you need in terms of specialist items e.g. pharmaceutical and electronic. In the more remote locations, the small local shops sell basic everyday items and can usually only handle money in small denominations.

Every main town in East Timor has a lively market with a wide array of colorful shops that sell local produce. Waterfront fruit stalls are very common and are mostly manned by friendly local women. Mangoes, papayas and bananas are always fresh. Haggling is unheard of, as you rarely see overpriced goods in local shops.

Coffee: Organically grown East Timorese coffee is among the best in the world. The coffee beans are known for their low acidity levels, which result in excellent tasting brews. The country also produces a wide variety of flavors, including the caffeine-rich Robusta. Make it a point to buy beans only in traditional markets, as grocery store stocks are mostly pre-ground.

Tais: Tais are hand-woven clothe made using traditional weaving techniques. They are a large part of the East Timor's cultural heritage and are customarily used for religious ceremonies, home decor and apparel. Historically, tais were the unit of exchange for livestock and other valuables. They come in many designs, styles and colors, influenced by either regional origins or familial heritage and ancestry. There is a large tais market in Dili where you can find authentic weavings sourced from all over the country. Local handicrafts like ethnic woodcarvings, embroidered fabrics, batik cloth, and traditional silver jewelry are also sold here.

Transportation

East Timor Taxis and Car Rental
Taxis are the best form of transportation within and around the main city in East Timor, especially if it's your first time visiting. Most drivers are willing to take you to far off coastal areas and attractions as long as you're willing to pay extra.

If you're looking for a more adventurous trip and don't mind driving in rough conditions, renting a car is an option. The lack of road signs may take you off the beaten path, but the scenery and hidden marvels of the small towns will more than make up for getting lost. Renting a four-wheel drive vehicle for off-road excursions is affordable, but make sure to always carry a valid driver's license or permit issued in East Timor or from your home country. A speed limit of 25 mph (40 kph) is imposed within Dili, though open roads allow you to go to 37 mph (60 kph). *Rentlo Car Hire* (+670-741-6982) is the rental provider in East Timor, specializing in recreational vehicles and passenger cars.

East Timor Water Taxis

In the past, Dili served as a main port for Pelni ships from Indonesia. However, this is no longer the case, and ferries are now only used to get to and from Atauro Island and the Oecussi Enclave. Jaco Island can also be reached by boat from Dili.

East Timor Trains and Buses

Land travel between towns and cities, as well as the main border to West Timor is mainly done by bus as there isn't any established rail system in the country. Cross-border buses offer direct services between Kupang (West Timor) and Dili. The Kupang-Dili route takes 12 hours and many minibus companies offer group or individual tickets. Check out *Leste Oeste Travel*, *Timor Travel* and *Paradise Travel* for prices and schedules.

Non-direct buses also operate from Dili to Atambua. The lines that run to the Batugade and Mota'ain border are cheap and the journey typically only takes three hours. You'll find buses that leave for Baucau from Rua Quinze de Outubro, near the roundabout in the municipal market.

Mikrolets are also a popular form of transportation from Dili to other parts of East Timor. These are vans that have been converted into shared passenger vehicles. They travel to Becora, Comoro, nearby suburbs, and beyond. Fares are cheaper than either bus or taxi.

Travel Tips

Language
Tetum and Portuguese are the two most common languages in East Timor, reflecting significant Portuguese influence. Variations of the Tetum dialect have developed throughout the years, with Tetun-Dili being the favored tongue. English and Indonesian are the main working languages as defined by the constitution, but more than 35 indigenous languages are spoken in many places around the country. About 90 percent of the population uses Tetum as their daily language.

Currency

East Timor uses the US dollar as its legal tender. US coins are widely accepted. Banks are predominantly found in Dili, along with ATMs. It is advised to bring cash and don't depend on plastic, as credit cards are only accepted in some hotels and a handful of restaurants in the capital city. ANZ bank has a branch which allows for overseas money transfers. If you are looking for a cheaper way to transfer money, try the Western Union in Dili. Bank Mandiri, a major bank in Indonesia, also has a branch in Dili near the Government Building. A Portuguese bank called Caixa Gera de Depositos has several locations within the country.

Time: GMT +9

Electricity
The power supply throughout East Timor can be erratic. Three-pronged plugs are standard, with electricity at 220V and 50Hz. US travelers using appliances from home will need to bring a transformer and plug adaptor.

Communications
The country code for East Timor is +670 despite the switch from Australian to its own network. The internet was only made accessible to the public in 2002, and is only available in the main city, Baucau, a few smaller cities. Timor Telecom has a monopoly on all

telecommunications in the country, from landlines to mobile phone and internet.

Duty-free
Visitors can bring up to 200 cigarettes and 2.25 liters of alcohol into the country without paying duty.

Tourist Office
Turismo de Timor-Leste (East Timor Government Tourism Office), Ministry of Development, Apartado 194, Dili, East Timor: +3-310-371 or +3-339-178, or www.turismotimorleste.com

Consulates in East Timor
United States Consulate, Dili: +670-390-324-684 Australia Consulate, Dili: +670-390-322-111 Great Britain Consulate, Dili: +670-390-723-1606 Canadian Consulate (c/o Canadian Embassy, Jakarta): +62-021-2550-7800 Brazilian Consulate, Dili: +670-332-1728 Ireland Consulate: +670-332-4880

Emergency
SOS Emergency Medivac: +61-2-9372-2468 UNPOL Emergency (Police): 112

Weather

Like most countries in the region, East Timor is governed by both a wet and dry season. The rainy period lasts from November to May, while the remaining months (June through October) mark dry weather. The average temperature throughout the year is 86°F (30°C), though it can get very cold at high altitudes.

Rains can be torrential during the wet season, which can cause frequent flooding, and may pose a problem for visits to remote areas of the country. The northern coast becomes particularly dry and parched during the dry season, so it is best to avoid north coast area when visiting during the warmer climate.

Best Time to Visit East Timor

Anytime is a good time to visit East Timor, temperature-wise, but make sure to avoid the wet months so storms don't ruin your trip. May through July is probably the nicest time to visit, when the climate is comfortable and the hills and fields are all abloom.

Holidays and Festivals

Though still a relatively young and recovering country, East Timor holidays and events include a number of cultural celebrations, including Christian and Islamic celebrations, as well as observances related to the long struggle for independence.

Festival of Culture and Food of Timor-Leste: Held early in the year (March), the annual Festival of Culture and Food of Timor-Leste aims to share the Timorese culture with the world. Expect traditional dances, music, and many other forms of entertainment, enhanced by good eats.

Independence Restoration Day: Observed May 20 as a public holiday, this day in 2002 marked the UN's transfer of sovereignty to the newly elected East Timor government. Festivities take place nationwide with Mass at church and tributes paid to those who fought for freedom.

Festival for Peace (Festa ba Dame): Held in June, the Festival for Peace is a series of shows and exhibits performed and organized by the youth who attend intensive art, multimedia, dancing, and music lessons at Ba Futuru. It aims to promote personal growth and improve the life of those living in conflict-prone areas of Dili, as well as those who are impacted directly or indirectly by violence.

Ramelau Cultural Festival: Named after the country's highest peak, the Ramelau Cultural Festival is the biggest cultural event held outside of the capital in East Timor. It is based in the Ainaro district and held late in the year usually in October. The three-day event of cultural pride honors Mount Ramelau, a symbol of Timorese pride and unity.

National Youth Day: November 12 marks the anniversary of the massacre of Santa Cruz, which occurred in Dili in 1991. A public holiday, this tragic day saw peaceful, pro-independence protesters massacred by Indonesian military forces.

National Heroes' Day: Observed on December 7, this public holiday pays tribute to the country's many heroes in the fight for independence while also remembering the day of the 1975 invasion of East Timor by Indonesia.

Food of East Timor

Cuisine of East Timor

In East Timor the gastronomy is mostly influenced by Southeast Asian foods and the Portuguese typical dishes from its period under Portuguese influence. Regional popular ingredients are pork, basil, vegetables, fish, rice, corn, tropical fruit and root vegetables.

Popular dishes in East Timor

As many other countries in the region the food is typical divided into two different categories: non-vegetarian and vegetarian. Since agriculture is one of the most important sectors in the country, the cuisine uses mainly rice (since its largely homegrown). Other types of main bases for the dishes of East

Timor are sweet potatoes, corn, cassava (type of mandioca) and taro. To add up to the base of every dish there is usually a vegetable component, also with home grown products such as cow-peas, onions, spinach and cabbage. In East Timor is common for the family to domesticate some sort of live stock, hence you know that this will also be a part of their cuisine. Commonly, you find the dishes combine pigs, poultry and goats.

Together with meat, fish also occupies a huge range of food (since after agriculture is the nations second biggest sector). Usually the fish is fried and prawns are considered a national delicacy. Below there are a couple of national dishes and links to their recipes in case you want to give it a try yourself at home before you eat the real food:

www.ingramcontent.com/pod-product-compliance
Lightning Source LLC
Chambersburg PA
CBHW031120080526
44587CB00011B/1049